When You Feel Insecure

Resources for Living

Andrew D. Lester
General Editor

When You
Feel Insecure

John P. Reed

Westminster/John Knox Press
Louisville, Kentucky

Scripture quotations from the Revised Standard Version of the Bible are copyrighted 1946, 1952, © 1971, 1973 by the Division of Christian Education of the National Council of the Churches of Christ in the U.S.A. and are used by permission.

Grateful acknowledgment is made for permission to quote in chapter 5 from *The Member of the Wedding* by Carson McCullers. Copyright 1946 by Carson McCullers. Copyright © renewed 1974 by Floria V. Lasky. Reprinted by permission of Houghton Mifflin Company.

Book design by Gene Harris

First edition

Published by Westminster/John Knox Press
Louisville, Kentucky

PRINTED IN THE UNITED STATES OF AMERICA

9 8 7 6 5 4 3 2 1

Library of Congress Cataloging-in-Publication Data

Reed, John P. (John Pershing), 1948–
   When you feel insecure / John P. Reed. — 1st ed.
      p.   cm. — (Resources for living)
   Bibliography: p.
   ISBN 0-664-25049-1

   1. Identification (Religion) 2. Self-respect—Religious aspects—
Christianity. 3. Security (Psychology) I. Title. II. Series.
BV4509.5.R44   1989   89-32569
158′.1—dc20   CIP

Contents

For
Linda,
Rachel, and J.P.,
my main coauthors in life

Preface

Time and again in my work as a pastoral counselor I hear the statement, "I feel so insecure," or the goal, "I want to be more sure of myself." It's a dangerous world out there! Most of us are beset by vague feelings of insecurity. Merely reading the morning newspaper, with its stories of Wall Street madness, world political upheaval, or earthquakes in California may stir up insecurities that haunt us throughout the day. The little things closer to home, however, are what really get to us: the sinking feeling of being too dependent on a spouse, consuming anxiety over career and job security, a vague fear that life just isn't going to pan out the way we had imagined. These are the expressions of insecurity addressed in this book.

No one can live life totally free of insecurity. I am convinced, however, that a deep and fairly consistent sense of security is attainable. Ironically, we are our own worst enemies in this matter. If we experienced life as depriving or dangerous when we were small, weak, and dependent, we now strive to recover security in two ways. First, we develop psychological defenses designed to make us less vulnerable. The problem is that these defenses become in our adult life the walls of a psychological prison that trap us and prevent our finding more reliable sources of security. Second, we institute an offensive policy of striking back at life. We repeat the past in our current relationships in order to control life so that we are never hurt again. Unfortunately, this policy simply leaves us feeling miserable because our efforts to control others inevitably backfire.

The purpose of this book is to help readers who feel insecure to identify and let go of destructive policies of defense and offense. You will be introduced to a new strategy for achieving security in life. You will learn in a logical progression that it is by remembering, mourning, and forgiving the past, letting go of negative defenses, accepting your healthy dependencies, and opening yourselves to new sources of goodness in life that security is achieved.

My own life has been a kind of pilgrim's progress from paralyzing insecurity to an increased sense of confidence and freedom from chronic fear. I still become afraid sometimes. Periods of stress or times of personal tragedy threaten to throw me back into the despair of insecurity, and at such times I am tempted to pull out some of my old defenses. The joy of being a pilgrim, however, is that growth and change are possible, and even a slow learner like me can meet life's challenges with new expressions of courage and creativity. This book describes the steps I found necessary for moving from insecurity to inner security. You can do this too.

Just as every life story has many authors, so does every book. This very fact of our mutual influence is one main basis for a sense of security. While they should not be held accountable for any weaknesses in these pages, several people have contributed greatly to the ideas set forth here. First and foremost among them are the individuals, couples, and families whom it has been my privilege to counsel. The stories of several of them are mentioned in this book, although the names are fictitious and the stories altered and simplified.

I am indebted to Joan Bush, Bob Cunningham, John Neill, Glenn Dorris, and Ray Wilkie, who encouraged me to write this book and made helpful suggestions regarding the manuscript. To my colleagues at the Samaritan Center in Lexington and to the Kilgore Samaritan Counseling Center in Louisville, I am grateful for stimulating dialogues that helped focus my thoughts on the topic of security. The singles of Calvary Baptist Church, Lexington, and the Facts of Life Forum of Second Presbyterian Church, Louisville, let me try my ideas on them in retreat settings and gave enormously helpful feedback.

Andrew D. Lester, editor for the series in which this volume appears, has been a longtime friend, colleague in ministry, mentor, and personal hero. His wise guidance has been both enjoyable to experience and essential so far as preparing a readable text is concerned. My wife, Linda, gave generously of encouragement and support, which is incredible when you consider that she was doing doctoral work at the same time and needed the word processor many of the times I was hogging it for this book. She and our daughter, Rachel, and son, J.P., are the main coauthors of my life and the major sources of my meaning, joy, and security. To them this book is dedicated.

1

"Where Are You, Norman Rockwell?"

When did you first realize you were insecure: as a young child? in adolescence? as a fledgling adult? What was the context and what were the contributing factors: an unstable family situation? problems at school? the dating scene?

What was the larger context? For many of us, the very world we live in serves as the backdrop for our insecurity. Our generation lives in a global village of televised wars, earthquakes, divorces, stock market crashes, and political terrorism. No wonder we're insecure! Even those of us who were fortunate enough to have a secure family life as children have had to contend with a complex and confusing world of change. When a seventeen-year-old girl justifies defying her parents' wish that she finish high school and go to college by saying, "What difference does it make? In ten years we'll all be nuked anyway!" you begin to get an idea of the global setting for our personal dramas. This young woman's insecurity, while stemming largely from family dynamics (her parents had recently been divorced), was aggravated by something going on in her larger world. This chapter takes a look at some of the social changes contributing to our sense of insecurity.

Crisis and the Loss of Innocence

During my first week in college, I experienced what I can only call, in retrospect, a mental crisis. I won't say mental breakdown, although I may have been closer to a collapse than I like to think. It was more of a late-adolescent mental storm, turbulent and frightening. I didn't know what was happening to me. Having had no experience of mental and emotional upheaval, I didn't have the sense to get help. I have often wondered since that time whether my early adult life might have been different had I sought out the campus chaplain or counselor. "Getting help" was not something one did in the pull-yourself-up-by-your-bootstraps Texan culture in which I grew up.

What was going on with me? First, I was seized by what the psychologists refer to as "separation anxiety." Although the college was only sixty miles from my home, it may as well have been sixty thousand. For a nineteen-year-old rugged individualist, this paralyzing homesickness was terribly embarrassing, so I admitted it to no one. Actually, I didn't really know anyone, which exacerbated my anxiety. I was agonizingly alone.

Separation anxiety is not all that uncommon among college freshmen. Like many others in my class, most of us strangers to one another, I was disoriented and missed the security of hearth and home. I also missed my girlfriend, who had gone to another college. Looking back, I realize that I was confronting more than the anxiety of leaving home. In effect I had left my old world behind and entered a strange new one.

During orientation week, the campus officials herded all freshmen into the auditorium one night to view the movie *Fail-Safe*. It was an early film dealing with the rising fear that our technology, coupled with Cold War tensions, could destroy the world. I'll never forget Henry Fonda playing the President having to make the awful decision to bomb New York City as a recompense to Russia for our accidentally bombing Moscow when our "fail-safe" defense system failed!

Orientation week at college was turning out to be terribly *dis-*orienting for a sheltered boy from suburbia. I went back to my dorm room and tossed and turned all night. For the next six weeks, night became day (I was afraid to fall asleep) and day became night. I barely kept up with my classes, and it is a wonder that I passed that first semester of college.

Like most baby boomers, I had grown up under the vague shadow of the mushroom cloud, during the era of bomb drills at school and neighbors building bomb shelters in their back yards. But the threat had never seemed real until that first week at college. My anxiety was not just a reaction to that movie or to living in a nuclear age. I was beginning to realize the complexity of all the changes that were taking place around me. It was as if college were saying, "John, you've lived a sheltered life. You don't know much about the real world. You've based your life on false securities and simplistic truths." For me, this occasioned a terrible crisis of identity and a trial of faith, crises I have been struggling to work through ever since.

As I said, I sought no help at the time. Somehow, by the grace of God, I muddled through. It was a time of confusion, of deep questioning and searching. The help came later, after college.

I can look back now on this college crisis as one of the most vitally important experiences of my life. Eventually, out of the dust and ashes of my adolescent belief system arose a new and ever enlarging worldview and an orienting faith equal to the complexity and insecurity of this world and adequate to deal with my own complexity and insecurity as an individual.

At the time, however, with the dawning realization of the nature of the world we live in came an equally troubling realization of how conflicted and insecure I was within myself. It had never occurred to me, for instance, that I possessed a deep rage and an equally deep distrust of people. I had always been a "good boy," sociable and well-liked. It would not come clear to me until much later that I was a highly defended and very controlling person, all symptoms of an underlying and pervasive insecurity.

In retrospect, I doubt that my story of lost innocence is very different from yours. I have had the privilege of hearing many other people recount similar journeys from what seemed the simple world of childhood to the complicated world of adulthood. Like you and me, they found themselves struggling not only with the insecurities instilled in them in childhood but with the social, historical, and political changes that contributed mightily to their personal insecurities. The point is, these are difficult times in which we live. As human beings, we are all creatures of the historical moment. Coming to terms with our personal insecurity necessarily involves, at least in part, coming to terms with the times in which we are living out our lives.

I remember Don, for instance, who was training to do pastoral psychotherapy under my supervision. Don had been serving in the army in Vietnam about the same time I was in my freshman year in college. His late-adolescent encounter with the real world was far more profound and devastating than my freshman year mini-breakdown had been. The black sheep of his strict Baptist family, Don had volunteered for duty, hoping to win the approval of "patriotic" parents. One day, as part of a military detail rounding up and transporting Vietnamese civilians out of a dangerous battle zone, he became impatient with a young mother who was clutching her baby and refusing to get on the wagon carrying civilians to safety. Dazed and wearied by the constant tension of guerrilla warfare in a booby-trapped country, Don was startled and horrified to find himself holding his bayonet at the baby's throat to pressure the woman into climbing on the wagon. As he handed the unharmed infant back to its mother, something inside Don shattered. He was never the same again. The world as he had known it had come unglued, and he was sickened. It was as if Don had momentarily fallen through an unexpected tear in the fabric of meaning that had heretofore governed his existence. It is a tribute to his personal strength and the heroism in his character that he was able to grab hold and get himself back into a meaningful world, yet this world—for him as for countless other veterans of war—was a radically different one.

After Don returned from Vietnam, there was no celebration. Had this soldier won his parents' blessing? No. In fact he learned from his sister that his mother had openly prayed that if Don did not get "saved" while in Vietnam she wanted God to "send him home in a wooden box." Can you imagine how Don felt about being so "loved" by his pious mother—a mother who was perhaps encapsulating herself in a simplistic view of life as protection against a frighteningly ambiguous world? In despair, Don joined a lawless motorcycle club. One day, while riding his motorcycle high in the mountains, he did have a religious conversion. His mystical "Rocky Mountain High" experience would not have been recognized as getting "saved" by his family, but it was real and life-changing for Don. He went to college and seminary and, when I met him, was training to be a chaplain and counselor.

In both his war experience and later as a Vietnam veteran, Don was struggling both with his wounds from childhood (terrible deprivations that underlay his adolescent delinquency) and with the social upheaval of his place in history (deprecation of his life-risking involvement in the Vietnam war). In one of our supervision sessions, the terrors he had bravely endured as a soldier so moved me that I stood and saluted him. The two of us stood at attention for what seemed like a long while, tears leaking from our eyes, and then we embraced. For Don, it was the blessing he had waited for but never gotten from his parents or from his country. For me, a guilty bystander whose only real involvement during the Vietnam years was in dormitory bull sessions and debates with my father, it was a healing participation in a soldier's journey. For both of us, it was a coming to terms with the insecurity of the time in which we live, with its clash between old absolutes and modern complexities.

A World Where Nothing Is Nailed Down (Including Us)

Overcoming personal insecurity is very difficult in this age because nothing is nailed down anymore. Our baby-boom generation has witnessed tremendous social change. The definitions of what it means to be a man or a woman, of what life should mean, and of what matters most in a hierarchy of values are all fluid, murky, and highly subjective.

Our generation, of course, confronts the same threats to security that have plagued all people of all times: natural catastrophe (flood, epidemic, earthquake, cancer), economic upheaval, political instability, and war. Our generation, however, has witnessed enormous social changes that are unique.

The Collapse of Authority

One of the things that most attracted me to my wife was the bumper sticker on her car: QUESTION AUTHORITY. I admired her panache and her refusal to be pigeonholed by narrow definitions of what it means to be a woman or by limiting and arbitrary expectations of what she could do or be as a person. I found her motto a refreshing alternative to that mystifying and depressing old bumper sticker, AMERICA: LOVE IT OR LEAVE IT, which seemed to presume that somewhere someone in the know had forever established what was, indeed, American and un-American. Questioning authority has seemed to me to be essentially American.

What both my wife and I have grimly realized as we attempt to rear our children in today's world is what social critics have been telling us for years, that a general collapse of all authority has occurred, not so much as a result of a healthy questioning of established values as from changes in the place and role of fathers and certainly from a deep suspicion of the credibility of those in authority. Vietnam, Watergate, Three Mile Island, the TV evangelism scandals, and other events have contributed to the erosion of authority and left scars of distrust and suspicion on the American psyche. Today's young corporate executive is less apt to play the ideal loyal company man or woman, given the publicized betrayals by some large corporations of his or her elder colleagues, laid off as they neared retirement. Overcoming personal insecurities is doubly difficult in a world plagued by a pervasive distrust of all authority.

Pluralism

Closely related to the collapse of authority is the fact of pluralism. Pluralism refers to the many competing ideologies, belief systems, and values that lobby for our allegiance and vie for the status of top authority in our lives. Returning to the bumper-sticker message QUESTION AUTHORITY, we can see our problem clearly when we ask, "Which authority do we question?" There are scores of value systems from which to choose. Many implicit but unarticulated values shape and mold us by way of television programming and advertising.

Religiously, we have gone from a nation with a Protestant majority to a nation where religions of all stripes abound and where new faiths and cults are born almost daily. The upside of this, of course, is that it makes us a diverse people undergirded in our diversity by a constitutional guarantee of religious freedom. The downside is that the pursuit of happiness, conceived in religious or moral terms, is a much less certain enterprise in a pluralistic world. How is one to determine what constitutes happiness when the norms for happiness are more apt to be dictated by Gallup polls than by moral or religious reflection?

With pluralism has come the loss of a common language of commonly held values, which renders public discourse cacophonous if not impossible. Many of us, bewildered by all the competing ideologies and lacking the anchor of abiding beliefs, are easily swayed by this fad or that, by what's in vogue in fashion, politics, or religion. Our only real freedom may be in our role as consumers, choosing this product over that for God knows what reason.

This pluralistic world is, I suggest, a ripe environment for personal insecurity. For most of us, if we're honest, the many competing notions of what's right and wrong, good and bad, coming our way daily actually paralyze us. The insecurity is like the insecurity we feel when a sure belief we hold to tenaciously is refuted or sorely challenged, but multiplied to the nth power.

The Loss of Transcendence

With the collapse of authority and with a pluralistic world has also come a loss in the sense of the transcendent. Theologian Edward Farley has said that pluralism has led to a "diminution in religious reality."[1] We are less certain of the validity of our belief, less certain that our word "God" refers to an actual reality. The power of belief is diminished. Despite what pollsters tell us about a pervasive belief in God in America, an abiding and life-changing belief in God appears to be rare.

Even where belief in God prevails, the vertical dimensions of faith have given way to horizontal ones. God is present in other people, or in nature, or in acts of love. Often the notion of God is employed in utilitarian ways. We invoke God's approval at the beginning of a sporting event. God is co-opted to validate this cause or that, be it liberal, conservative, or fundamental. In this horizontal religion at its worst, God becomes the mascot for political and economic agendas, from the Moral Majority's conservatism to the Ayatollah's fundamentalist regime. In our time, the sense of God as transcendent, as holy Other, as the absolute Mystery who cannot be used but only worshiped, is slipping away.

This slippage with regard to transcendence is a troubling

development. It contributes to our insecurity and makes achieving a secure sense of self an enormous challenge. The very validation and preservation of our selfhood depends on the existence of a transcendent source and reference point. Most of us cannot accept the notion of God as a bearded old man sitting on his throne just outside the city limits of the universe. Where, then, is God?

Perhaps all the self-consciousness and obsessive activity related to finding and actualizing oneself in our society is due, in no small measure, to this loss of a palpable sense of the transcendent. The accompanying loss of interest in the afterlife has put all the pressure on this present life to produce the stuff that makes for meaningful selfhood. Is it possible that this loss of transcendence puts an unbearable expectation on such mundane things as marriage? Marriage, or the marriage partner, is being asked to supply what in former times would have been asked only of God.

The Battle of the Sexes

In my life and work it has increasingly come home to me that very much in human fulfillment depends on the quality of relationships between men and women. This is not new. The fact that the sexes have experienced each other as deadly enemies as well as allies in life's journey, as the objects of hate as well as of love, is well known. This generation, however, has witnessed never-before-confronted sexual agendas in every arena of life, from home to marketplace to the halls of justice and power.

The same baby boomers who have never lived a day of their lives outside the shadow of the mushroom cloud have also never been far removed from the tremendous sexual revolution that has been occurring since the end of World War II. How have we coped with these social transformations?

The Women's Liberation Movement has ushered in incredible changes in relationships between men and women and has invited resistance and criticism as well as applause and celebration. Regardless of one's view of feminism, no one remains unaffected by it. In working to help both men and women to grow individually and in relationship, I regard the feminist movement as a basically welcome historical development. The liberation of women from the bondage of constricting definitions of selfhood is consonant with the overall liberating message of the gospel. However, the movement has contributed to deep insecurities in both sexes.

In my practice I have observed women who opt for more traditional roles, struggling to combat feelings of shame that they are somehow falling short of society's expectations. They often face pressure from family and peers and find themselves dealing with not-so-subtle put-downs of their choices. On the other hand, I see many women struggling to do it all, to balance the demands of career and family, too often without the support they need from the men in their lives. These women are exhausted and are often secretly berating themselves for not measuring up to some impossible standard.

Our generation of women grew up with one set of models for womanhood and have had to adapt to tremendous changes and to multiple models. These changes have complicated women's relationships with their mothers as well as with their men. Achieving a secure sense of selfhood is a terribly difficult challenge for women. We are still in flux on this issue. Uncertainty reigns with regard to what it means to be authentically male or female in these times.

The men I see are also greatly affected and are often extremely resistive to the changes, even when they consciously think of themselves as "liberated." Many men have been made to feel terribly insecure by changes in "their" women. A recurring marital problem is that of the wife who wants to go back to school or enter the job market and the husband who digs in his heels because he dreads losing something important. Just what that "something important" is he may not be able to articulate, but shifts in roles and in the balance of power required by these changes often strain marriage to the breaking point.

Our generation has witnessed frightening upheaval in the institution of marriage itself. Divorce has become a common American phenomenon. The "blended family," along with the single-parent family, may actually become more typical of families in the near future. Trends in marriage have left a legacy of insecurity for men, women, and children. Countless adolescents repeatedly speak of their fear of marriage, a fear usually born of observation of the pervasive facts of their parents' conflict and divorce. They know that in this matter of commitment, of being man and woman in cooperative relationship, even in love, nothing is certain.

Changing patterns in attachment and commitment between men and women have been unsettling to us all. These changes are caused, in large part, by our basic attitudes toward dependency, to the fact of our needing others, which I will discuss a little later.

The collapse of authority, pluralism, the loss of transcendence, and the new battle of the sexes are only some of the forces and changes that continually chip away at our security. I have alluded to the threat to our sense of security aroused by living in a nuclear age.[2] New developments in technology, and the rootlessness and breakdown of the extended family, also work against a sense of security. Many other complex forces also work against us. To put it mildly, we aren't living in Disneyland! This is a very complicated world, one in which it often seems that nothing is stable or constant, including us.

Our Dependency Phobia

One of the greatest contributors to problems of insecurity in our time and culture is our dependency phobia. Americans dread dependency like the plague. I'm not just referring to the fear most of us have of growing old and becoming physically incapacitated and dependent on others for our care, though that is certainly one of its manifestations. What I am mainly referring to is the pervasive negative attitude toward dependency of any kind that is so deeply ingrained in the American psyche, an attitude which, without our realizing it, undercuts the security we so desperately want and strive to attain.

In our craving for autonomy and self-sufficiency, we downplay or even lose sight of the very human striving for dependency that makes attachment to secure moorings possible. Often, we mean by the adjective "insecure" that a person lacks the capacity to govern himself or herself with confidence. The need for approval or support from someone else (a spouse, a parent, even a child) is so strong it is clear that authority over this person's life is located externally. Autonomy, the capacity for self-governance, is certainly a major element in becoming a secure self.

Autonomy, however, is problematic in American society. American culture and American psychology have idealized independence, exalting it to the level of a virtue of mental health to the neglect and even to the disparagement of dependency. In American life and thought, "dependency" is a dirty word, almost always conceived as something negative, equated with weakness. Robert Bellah, in his book *Habits of the Heart,* describes and assesses the characteristically American exaltation of autonomy and illuminates the difficulties into which this absolutizing of autonomy has gotten us. With what I call this idolatry of autonomy has come a loss of the capacity for true community. With it, the burden of self-definition is totally on the shoulders of the individual. Furthermore, with this exaltation of autonomy has come an erosion of authentic attachment and of abiding commitment to others. Bellah captures our dilemma when he says:

> We strongly assert the value of our self-reliance and autonomy. We deeply feel the emptiness of a life without sustaining social commitments. Yet we are hesitant to articulate our sense that we need one another as much as we need to stand alone, for fear that if we did we would lose our independence altogether.[3]

We are not merely hesitant but downright scared of acknowledging our need for others. Being in a need-satisfying system of relationships is one of the main ways we achieve a sense of security, but our fear of this neediness may lead us unwittingly to sabotage our very efforts. All relationships become treacherous to the extent we fear that being in them can rob us of our independence. Unfortunately, the psychology-minded culture we live in too often reinforces this problem when it reflects this climate of dependency phobia.

We owe the renowned psychologist Erik Erikson a great debt for clarifying the importance of achieving autonomy in the child's development.[4] Autonomy is important. Achieving it is a necessary building block for all future development. The building block necessary for achieving autonomy, however, is what Erikson called basic trust, which he linked to the dependency state. Autonomy grows out of something even more basic, a trust in the fundamental dependability of life and relationship. Other psychologists, however, have picked up and overstressed autonomy to the neglect of dependency. This lopsided attitude has, perhaps, been most unfair to women. Carol Gilligan and other women psychologists have recently emphasized the neglected virtue in dependency and the capacity for attachment.[5] Men have also suffered from the depreciation of dependency and the virtual exclusion of it from any definition of masculinity.

We have such a hard time accepting our dependency because we equate it with weakness and helplessness. Few of us want to be thought of as weak. Most of us can recognize ourselves in the blanket-clutching Linus of the *Peanuts* comic strip. Like Linus, we yearn for security in a world that often seems all too confusing and unsafe. We laugh at Linus in part because we identify with him. In Linus we get a glimpse of that insecure child within us, but we do not really want to be like him. We want to be strong and self-reliant. In our fear of acknowledging those points at which we are weak and in need of others' support, we tend, like Linus, to find some substitute focus for our anxiety, some inadequate and alternative means of reassuring ourselves. Our security blankets assume many forms, and some of them are quite destructive. They suffocate life rather than providing a secure basis for growth.

In chapter 5, I will attempt to show how a new attitude toward dependency is possible and even necessary if we are to overcome our insecurity. The question is not whether we will be dependent; we all are. The question is, How shall we find dependable foundations, within and without, for our deep and valid dependency strivings?

The Aching Nostalgia for a Simpler World

Given the burden of autonomy, the great burden of having to erect our personality all by our lonesome on what seems a foundation of quicksand, where nothing can be nailed down, we may become seized by a nostalgia for "the way we were." Tom was a thirty-eight-year-old professional man who came for counseling because of chronic feelings of insecurity. He was at the top of his profession and was in a basically good marriage, his second. Still, he was plagued by insecurity, which in turn caused him to be self-absorbed, a tendency he intensely disliked in himself. He lamented that he could no longer find meaning in the simple truths of his small-town Disciples of Christ upbringing.

Tom was a self-diagnosed "religiously disoriented Yuppie of the eighties." During the course of counseling, he wrote a poem entitled, "Where Are You, Norman Rockwell?" which eloquently expressed his nostalgic yearning for a simpler time, for the 1950s when Ozzie and Harriet reigned and when family and extended family seemed invulnerable as they gathered for Thanksgiving dinner. Tom attended church but felt no power in his belief or relevance to his problem of insecurity. Like many of us, he was confused by all the competing ideas of what it means to be a successful person, the mixed messages about personal success coming from Madison Avenue, Wall Street, Harvard, Hollywood, and all the other headquarters of authority that vie for our loyalties alongside the church.

While happy in his marriage to an intelligent, caring, and ambitious career woman, Tom was still haunted by ghosts of anxiety from his previous marriage to a woman who left him because she was climbing the career ladder and needed "room to grow." He feared becoming too dependent on his present wife, despite the fact that she was spontaneous in both giving and receiving nurture and gave no evidence of feeling oppressed by his emotional needs.

Tom's main concern was that he knew he had become quite self-absorbed. He sensed that he was taking more from his marriage than he was giving. Isn't there a voice of warning in each of us—frequently muffled, of course—that tells us we could lose those we need if our loving is not really addressing their needs?

The other and more troubling facet of Tom's self-centeredness was his own self-contempt. Whether or not his wife could live with him the way he was, he was having great difficulty living with himself. He was not the loving and sacrificing person he wanted to be. He was not living up to his ideal view of himself as an involved member of his community. He was not giving back to life the way he thought he should. His insecurity had made him self-absorbed. This happens. When we use up all our psychic energy just to stay afloat, we seldom notice the guy who is drowning, much less have energy left over to help.

Most of all, Tom was yearning and searching for something to sustain him, a power or a reference point greater than himself. He wanted to transcend himself, yet, like the rest of us, found himself in a world where self-transcendence is a vanishing capacity. He wanted an orienting faith, but, like us, he was bewildered by a host of competing ideologies and life-styles. The authorities, the heroes, the mentors in living had all disappeared. "Where are you, Norman Rockwell?" he wondered nostalgically.

I admired Tom for his openness and searching and drew inspiration and courage from his valiant struggle to come to terms with himself. As children of this age of uncertainty, he and I had much in common.

Tom is like a lot of us, though he may have been more zealous in his quest for answers. He tried many things. He was professionally successful. He traveled a lot, drove a sexy sports car, and even tried one of those survivalist weekends to prove himself. He yuppied it up with the best of us but continued to have a nagging sense of insecurity and an aching nostalgia for something simpler, something more basic. We shall return to Tom later to see how he shed some of the false securities with which he had blanketed himself.

False Security Blankets

While there are countless ways we attempt to soothe the emotional stress of living in an ambiguous world, four misguided external methods seem to be gaining popularity. The current trend toward achieving security in these ways is cause for concern. These methods promise security, but not only do they fail to guarantee security, they may actually aggravate our insecurity. In short, they are false security blankets. Furthermore, they all involve a kind of warping of our otherwise healthy dependency strivings. They do this by removing dependency strivings from the realm of interpersonal relationships and by diverting those needs to something impersonal. That is one main reason they fail. Our insecurities are fundamentally interpersonal. The answers to our insecurities are, likewise, deeply interpersonal.

In chapters 2 and 3 I will describe some of the *internal* methods we employ to reassure ourselves and to defend against insecurity, methods that also usually fail. Here I wish to identify four *external* methods. These four false security blankets are materialism, healthism, addiction, and religious absolutism.

Materialism

Madonna is singing for several generations, not just her own, when she sings "I'm a Material Girl." Something has gone awry in our culture. The American Dream of personal achievement by way of hard work has deteriorated into an insistence on instantaneous wish fulfillment. The noble notions of citizenship and making a contribution to society appear to have given way to a mentality of private consumerism and special interests. General Motors would not be too far off if it included the bumper sticker BORN TO SHOP as a standard feature on its new cars. We are all caught up in the materialism of this age.

I have little patience with those who only want to moralize about the selfishness of the me generation. That today's college student thinks more about his or her earning capacity than about righting the wrongs of society may be irksome to many of the sixties generation, but it does not call for knee-jerk judgmentalism. It is, rather, an occasion for sadness and soul-searching. The sixties generation itself is not exempt from the same materialistic tendencies.

The really startling fact about today's materialism is that it has less to do with temptation than it does with necessity. This is especially the case with young people in adolescence or young adulthood. Those who grew up in the sixties are more apt to be aware of an inner conflict between their material wants and their ideals. This is not merely a function of maturity, however. It is because they have a memory of that era of the flower child, of idealism, social activism, and the two-fingered peace sign, just as their parents have a memory of the Great Depression, of World War II rations, of patriotism and self-restraint. That some of today's young people lack an appreciation for old-fashioned virtues such as deferred gratification is not cause for moralistic finger-wagging. It is the occasion for sorrow and a searching for understanding of what underlies the urgent materialism of these times. All of us, young and old, are caught up in the current tide of fascination with wealth. The young simply hold up a mirror for the rest of us. The TV advertisers have captivated us all with the promise of security if we use this product or that.

The materialism that is so prevalent in this age has less to do with temptation than with cynicism. It is reflective of a deep cynicism about the future. It is the result of the loss of transcendence. The present is all there is, and this designer dress or that new Volvo is the only reliable answer to my insecurity. Those things will make me popular or powerful. If I win the lottery, look out; I'm home free!

It is not the desire for material security per se that I am referring to here, but the prevailing attitude that a thick stock portfolio and a closet full of designer clothes will solve one's deepest security needs. This attitude, part of the ethos of this age, borders on religious belief, albeit a belief more inherited than chosen. Perhaps the loss of transcendence, the loss of a robust and voluntary belief in the vertical dimensions of life, does leave us all stuck in the flat earth of materialism, hence our homage to material things and to those who have them.

In an age that has lost a palpable sense of the transcendent, we are in jeopardy of witnessing the eclipse of personal relationship by materialism. When we grow bored or run out of things to say to one another, we can always jump in the car and cruise the shopping centers. Mall shopping becomes a kind of anesthetic for the pains and demands arising out of our dependent relationships. It is easier to relate to things than to people. In a world where nothing is solid or certain, we are apt to turn to material things, which seem to supply a sense of tangible reality and security.

Healthism

Physical health is a good thing, a worthy pursuit. "Healthy mind in a healthy body" is a commendable motto for living, but in our society physical fitness has become an end in itself. The thin, tanned, muscular body as the object of worship has spawned a billion-dollar health industry, from the aerobics group that meets in the local church to posh health clubs, fitness centers, and tanning salons.

Personal security is the result of a beautiful, physically fit body, preach the new health gurus. I would not dare to contradict such a physical fitness institution as Jane Fonda. She looks terrific, and her self-discipline is admirable. The whole movement, however, has aggravated rather than solved our insecurity. Can one ever be thin enough?

I do not intend to discourage anyone from having a good workout or from setting realistic goals for losing weight, firming up, and getting in shape. Often, in psychotherapy, examining health patterns and establishing physical health plans are essential components to achieving emotional and interpersonal well-being. But this always occurs in a larger context and almost always is linked to deeper issues of dependency and to the recovery of transcendence.

As a means to a greater end, the health consciousness that flourishes today is a welcome development. As an "ism," a one-sided ideology of life, it becomes an idolatry and loses the capacity to deliver true inner security. We have come a long way from the days when we watched our mothers dutifully obeying Jack La Lanne's instructions to "bend and stretch." Is it possible that our obsession with fitness masks the deep insecurity of a people who have little tangible to work on beyond our own bodies?

Addiction

Without question, drug and alcohol addiction have become an alarmingly pervasive problem in American culture. Is there a link between massive addiction and the social, family, and individual insecurities of these times? I think so. The many addictions that plague our society can be understood as the result of a lopsided individualism and the loss of dependency values and of community. In a world of transient relationships, of ephemeral values, of kaleidoscopic changing images passing across the television screen, people long to be attached to something substantial, and so we have substance addiction.

Addiction means "to belong to" or "to be the slave of another," but as human beings we must belong to something. It is our nature. In a world that often appears too complicated, too confusing, too lonely, too stressful—in short, too undependable—we are prone to turn to a chemical substance, be it nicotine, caffeine, cocaine, or alcohol, particularly if that substance promises to answer one of two questions. First, does taking the substance help us to feel substantial? When we feel empty inside, when we feel ourselves to be hollow, dim shadows of ourselves, a substance that inflates us momentarily or heightens our senses can be very appealing. For a little while, we can feel as if we are "really there." Second, does the chemical substance help us escape into another "there"? If being in our real "there" of life, our real situation, is too stressful or painful, a drug that promises to numb the pain or take us away from it can be quite tempting. And by the millions we are so tempted.

Nevertheless, addiction does not provide the inner security it promises. It is a false security blanket. It destroys life and relationship. It simply doesn't work.

Religious Absolutism

A final false security blanket is a certain absolutizing approach to religious faith. I am not referring to religion itself but to a skewing that occurs in certain expressions of religious belief or, for that matter, in any ideological approach to human experience.

What do I mean by the term religious absolutism? I mean expressions of religious faith that attempt to deny or ignore the ambiguities of life. Human experience is fraught with ambiguities and uncertainties. Religious absolutizers try to restore a sense of security by denying this fact and by lifting up their own viewpoint to the status of law or divine truth.

We live in an age in which having faith and living out of that faith is difficult. Our religious commitments are challenged not only by such age-old problems as suffering (if there is a loving and just God, why do bad things happen to good people?) but also, now, by science and pluralism and, even more insidiously, by the vast changes in selfhood resulting from the hyperindividualism of this culture. The American spirit of independence, having been pushed to an irrational extreme, unbalanced by any regard for dependence, has resulted in a new self that is at once imperial and hopelessly disoriented.

The rise in religious absolutism can be understood as an effort on the part of growing numbers of well-intentioned people to reorient the self, albeit one that fails to comprehend both the complexities of our modern world and, I think, the deep roots in religious intuition of personal security. It fails, furthermore, to the extent that it shares the characteristically American aversion to dependence, to any hint of what might be called weakness. Yet religious absolutism, with its simple absolutes, is an alluring alternative in a pluralistic and ambiguous social and moral world.

Religious absolutizers act as if they can eradicate pluralism, the sexual revolution, the collapse of authority, secularism, and other sources of religious doubt simply by embracing certain ideological absolutes. It is as if they say to themselves, "The ambiguities of this world frighten me. I don't like them. Therefore, I will impose on this complex world my own simple and infallible viewpoint and support it with scripture that defends my own definition of what God wants and how God works in the world." Such persons endeavor to eliminate all doubt. Absolutist religion is intolerant of doubt and ambiguity. Love is absolutized and hate is denied or externalized. "Hate is out there in other people. It can't exist in me!"

Religious absolutism fails in its effort to "secure" security because we cannot eliminate all doubt or will away the ambiguities of life. Recently, a young seminarian came for counseling because of a series of panic attacks related to overwhelming doubt of the existence of God. In his student pastorate, he experienced paralyzing attacks of anxiety on Saturday nights, before he was to preach on Sunday. The pulpit was the only place he felt secure in his faith. The preaching act restored him temporarily. "If I don't find some basis for security, I'm going to explode!" he told me in our first session. Although he was nostalgic for the security of his conservative Baptist upbringing, he knew he could not roll back the clock or forget that he was a child of the age of pluralism, relativism, and the loss of transcendence. How would he regain a persuasive sense of the reality of God?

I can certainly identify with his quandary. I recall the latter days of college and my early years of seminary, when I vacillated between the certainties of my fundamentalist roots and the simultaneous appeal and intimidation of existentialist theology. I went through a period of being extremely defensive, especially about psychology. Many religious absolutists are wary of psychology, regarding it as humanistic and therefore ruinous to faith. I once shared with a fellow seminarian my disdain for the prolific writings (none of which I had yet read) of one of our professors of religious psychology. Ironically, it was in my first class with that same professor, Wayne E. Oates, that I first began to experience some healing of my deep wounds and to gain some reassurance about the validity of my faith and calling. I would not be writing this book about overcoming insecurity had it not been for the influence of this man and his faith perspective on my life. In the final chapters of this book, I will elaborate on how to find security without resorting to religious absolutism.

Is there any religious absolute upon which we can build a faith? Is there any belief or way of approaching faith that can nail us down, make us secure in ourselves and in our relationships, without becoming a religious absolutism? Is anything absolute, or is everything relative? I believe there is a way to relate to religious absolutes without becoming an absolutizer and will discuss this later. Genuine inner security is achievable and does involve a religious outlook. To understand how this is possible, we need to know more about what makes us tick. In the next two chapters, I will focus on the internal nature of our insecurity, on its psychology, and on the internal methods for achieving security we tend to employ.

Questions for Reflection

1. Several social forces and changes have been identified in this chapter as comprising the context of our insecurity: the collapse of authority, pluralism, the loss of transcendence, changes in the family, the women's movement, and the hyperindividualism of American culture. Which of these do you consider to be the greatest contributor to personal insecurity? What others would you add to the list?

2. When and how did you lose your innocence regarding the complexities and insecurities of the modern world? How was your faith affected by this loss of innocence?

3. Which false security blankets are you tempted to use? What others would you add to the list of four in this chapter?

4. How do you view dependency? Is it a positive or negative factor in relationships? Upon what or whom do you depend most for your security?

2

Fear and the Danger of Attachment

One of the great ironies of life is that the very thing we need most, secure relationships with significant others, can also be one of life's greatest dangers. Why? Because the very people whose love we most need—our parents, our spouse, even our child—are also capable of hurting us deeply. They can hurt us by rejecting us, by ignoring us, by misunderstanding us, by using us, by judging us, and in a thousand other ways. This chapter explains fear, the emotional component of insecurity, and its relationship to our dependency and need for attachment.

Mary's Compromise with a No-Win World

When Mary first entered psychotherapy, I thought she was one of the most frightened people I had ever met. She sat stiff as a board, her eyes glazed with fear. As she began to unfold her life story, I understood why she was afraid. Mary sought counseling as a last-ditch effort to get help before following through on her plans to end her life. In her thirty-six years of life, she had never felt at home. "I do not belong here on this earth," was her frequent refrain.

Those who have been most deeply wounded in life often have much to teach the rest of us. Mary's case may seem an extreme one, for her story, at points, is a living nightmare of chronic fear and insecurity. However, in the extremities of her struggle, Mary holds up a mirror for the rest of us. If we can muster the courage to look into that mirror, we will catch a glimpse of our own frightened selves. We may even gain some insight into the nature of our insecurities in light of our own dangerous attachments.

Mary had grown up on a divorce ranch in Nevada during the days when a mere six-week residency was required in that quick-divorce state. She spent her days surrounded by guests of the ranch, most of whom were people in a state of emotional upheaval. Mary's own family life was grim. Her father, a frustrated artist, managed the lodge as a way to make ends meet and to support his real love, art. He wanted sons and was openly disappointed that Mary, his second daughter, was a girl. He seemed to resent the drain of having children at all. Mary's mother, owing to painful losses in her own childhood as well as her preoccupation with her moody husband's occasional wanderings, was a very insecure and emotionally distant mother.

Mary could recall tumultuous periods in her early life. Her parents' method of dealing with Mary's emotional outbursts was to put her in a cold shower or threaten to leave her. There was little real love, the kind a child needs in order to feel secure and build any sense of self, not to mention self-esteem. Mary reached despair at an unusually early age. She recalls, as early as age five, retreating often to the bathroom, where she would hear a mocking voice inside her saying, "All you do is get born, grow up, get married, have kids, grow old, and die. If that's all there is, why live? There's nothing to this life." Like so many deeply wounded persons, Mary had barely gotten started with life when, because her world failed to respond to her normal yearning to be loved, she was saying, "Stop the world, I want to get off."

Mary's adolescence was even stormier. She had arrived at puberty without really ever being allowed to be a little girl. She wasn't ready for the emerging expectations of young adulthood. There was still no one in her life who offered any genuine understanding. She was simply regarded as a "difficult daughter."

Mary became increasingly isolated from family and peers. She was angry and frightened, but her anger always met with disapproval. She turned it on herself in self-loathing. She would retreat to her bathroom, look at herself in the mirror, pull her hair, and scream at the face in the mirror, "I hate you! I hate you!" Despite all this mental anguish, her natural giftedness could not be totally squelched. She was valedictorian of her class.

Mary's story reads like a documentary of the social and political tumult of the sixties and early seventies. From Haight Ashbury to the Newark riots to Kent State, Mary was there. She partially overcame her sexual inhibitions when she became involved in what she described as "the whole sexual political thing," but she only allowed herself to be intimate with men she really didn't care about. This was her compromise with her own sexual needs and the world of men. Whenever she started feeling something for one of her lovers she would pull back and move on, particularly after she had been dumped by a Vietnam draft dodger to whom she'd been engaged.

After a stint with Students for Democratic Action in Newark, she wound up in a love triangle with an attorney who had gone to work at Kent State following the debacle there and his mistress. She was simultaneously involved with a man she thought of as a psychic, who introduced her to psychedelic drugs. One evening he gave her LSD and left her alone in his apartment. She lay down beside the fireplace, the mantel of which was decorated like an altar of worship. She remembered hearing Orson Welles's famous "War of the Worlds" rebroadcast and feeling terrified, as though she were coming unglued. Later, she heard gospel music from the radio and was overwhelmed by what she described as a certain awareness of the reality of God. For the next several days she experienced a pervading sense of inner peace that she had never before known.

From that point on, Mary began a spiritual quest. Her sense of inner tranquillity was short-lived, but she persisted in reading the Bible, and moved from one mystic cult to another, never really finding a lasting place. She adopted a basically ascetic and celibate life-style. She connected more with religious ideas and practices than with people. For all her efforts at finding God and thereby recovering that moment of inner peace which had since eluded her, Mary could not escape her anger at a God who had allowed her to be so wounded and deprived. More importantly, she had come to identify God as the source of that inner voice which had always said, "You don't belong here on this earth." Mary's emerging faith became contaminated by a deep suspicion that God, if not an illusion, was at best a capricious trickster. At this point, and in this radically insecure state of mind, Mary came for psychotherapy.

Mary was a true child of this insecure age who experienced life as putting her in a double bind. She needed people in order to develop her own identity and sense of worth. Yet she also felt this need was immanently dangerous. From early in life, Mary had experienced the world as undependable and her dependence on her parents as profoundly threatening to her being as a person. This threat carried over into virtually every other relationship, so she avoided depending on anyone outside herself. She strove to be self-sufficient but failed to find an adequate foundation for her identity. Instead, in her inner world, she found chaos. In her outer world she drifted from radical politics to free sex, drugs, and religion, from experience to experience, person to person, but never truly connected with anyone.

Mary continued to search for love outside herself, but in a compromised manner. She never allowed herself really to open to being loved because, in her mind, that also meant risking more hurt and disappointment, which she believed she could no longer bear. She anesthetized her feelings whenever she feared someone was getting too close. At a time in the course of our work together when she was beginning to feel awkwardly dependent on me, she reproached me and herself with the reminder, "I can leave any relationship and never feel anything!" Even God could not be trusted. As a protection against the ultimate threat to her being of God's rejection, Mary substituted knowledge about God for direct relationship to God.

In this no-win world of God and people, Mary had struck an unworkable compromise. She had withdrawn into some inner sanctuary, but even there she was besieged by powers from her past. There was no solace to be found inside. She had to be eternally on guard, and this had become terribly wearisome. Mary realized that chronic insecurity can be exhausting. Her suicidal thoughts were the result of world-weariness, of life-tiredness. She wanted to go to sleep and never wake up, yet she feared that she might actually die before having really lived.

Your Song Haunts Us, Barbra Streisand

In the movie musical *Funny Girl,* Barbra Streisand captivated us with the sentimental song "People," the lyrics of which captured our ideal for relationships. The song tells us we are lucky if we realize our need for others. But the lyrics also touch on reality. Something happens to us in life between childhood and adulthood. Adult pride takes over, dictating that we conceal from the world the deep needs inside. What happens to our needy inner child that causes it to go into hiding?

People Who Depend on People

We begin life in a state of absolute dependence. We are fragile creatures, unable at the outset to do anything for ourselves except those things our autonomic nervous system controls, such as breathing. Even then, things can go wrong. We depend totally on mother, father, and other caretakers for our physical survival needs. Perhaps more importantly, we depend totally on them for our emotional needs. To become fully human, we need other people. We depend on our relationships with significant others in order to build up our own unique identity, to become our own true self. No one can achieve a sense of self in an emotional and relational vacuum. We are constituted by our relationships. This is how we become persons.[1]

If we have received fairly good mothering and fathering, we experience the world as a safe, reliable place.[2] Being absolutely *dependent* is OK in a *dependable* emotional environment. Good enough parenting will do; if our every need were responded to perfectly, we would never learn to do for ourselves and make ourselves feel secure. If our home environment provides consistency and predictability of care, we are able to make the transition from an infantile state of absolute dependence to a mature state of interdependence with others. We have the resources to feel emotionally secure.

Being emotionally secure does not mean that one does not need people. On the contrary, emotionally secure individuals recognize their need for others. They know they remain relatively dependent on other people—family members, friends, colleagues—in order to grow in self-concept. Because they experienced a good-enough initial experience of the interpersonal world, they are not threatened by this need for others. They are not undone by dependency, nor do they have to hide their need behind a layer of adult pride. They are those lucky people Barbra Streisand sings about. This is because they can depend on themselves as well as others.

People Who Hurt and Are Hurt by People

We don't have to experience the kind of wounding in childhood that Mary endured to understand that people can hurt people. Usually it is people who have themselves been hurt who in turn hurt others in their lives, sometimes intentionally but most often without intending to or even realizing what they are doing.

The True and the False Self Each of us, I believe, comes into this world already possessing the rudiments of a true self, which, if nurtured properly, flourishes and grows. This true self, also called our central core, our real self, or our inner child, is that authentic, spontaneous, creative, communicative essential center of our unique being.[3] Even in healthy development, we tend to keep our true self private and hidden, revealing it only in the context of creative pursuits or in a trusting relationship. We also develop a public self, which is the socially adapted image we present to the world. This split self is natural. The public self is not phony. We compose it by drawing from characteristics and qualities in our culture, but it bears our unique stamp. However, it does not express our essential depth, which we reserve for special revelation.

If we suffer too much hurt and emotional deprivation in our earliest relationships, there are two very unfortunate results. First, we are apt to withdraw our true self altogether from the world. We put it in cold storage somewhere in the deep recesses of our being, waiting doubtfully for a better world, one which might be more receptive to us. But once this occurs, we seldom open ourselves to that possibility. We have erected too many defenses against trusting the world again. Second, we construct

in place of our true self a false self, with which we come to
identify. This is our fear-ridden self. It is conformist and other-
directed. Our false self tries to achieve security by being whatever we think our important others need us to be in order for
them to feel secure.

This often happens with children whose parents are divorcing. They feel it is no longer safe to be their true, spontaneous
selves, lest in spontaneity they wreak further damage to the
family structure upon which they have depended for their security. Often, a child will identify with the structure itself, feeling
himself or herself to be the glue that will somehow hold things
together. Other children may protest and even rage against the
threat of loss of their true self which their parents' divorcing can
pose. They act out at school or at home and are labeled "problem children." Parents who lobby for their children's loyalty
during this time only make matters worse. This puts the child's
true self in an intolerable situation so its only recourse is to
withdraw from any real interaction with the world.

Certainly Mary went through a similar process. By age five
her true self was locked deep inside. The protests of toddler-
hood had been cold-showered into submission, and now she
was a depressed but adapted false self who no longer had any
reason to live. Her true self emerged from its cocoon once
when she was eleven, when at a family gathering someone
asked her what she wanted for Christmas and she blurted out
in anguish, "I only want the love of Christ to be here in our
home!" Her cry met with awkward silence from this irreligious
family, who had no inkling of what she was really asking for,
and her true self crept dejectedly back to its hiding place and
double-bolted the door.

It took a long time in psychotherapy for Mary to trust enough
to reveal her true self again, and it first appeared in this dream:

> I was in a room with my mother. I was feeling uneasy. A man
> was sitting on the floor across from us. He was a caring,
> accepting, loving person. I went and sat beside him. I felt I
> was married to him. He put his arms around me. He touched
> my stomach to feel the baby kicking inside me. I felt peaceful,

as if this were where I was supposed to be. My mother said my father was coming to see this man's art work. I felt good.

Mary regarded the kind artist in the dream as a symbol of me and her leaving her mother's side to join me as evidence of her tentative new trust in me. Her true self had not yet appeared, but there was the promise of that symbolized in terms of pregnancy and birth. It suggested that her true self would need to undergo rebirth, to start anew from the very beginning.

A kind of rebirth did occur during the course of my work with Mary. Just how this occurred, and how she achieved a sense of security, will be described in chapter 4.

Separation and Transition While infants can experience real terror, it is toddlers, young children who are beginning to separate and differentiate from their parents, who are often ridden by chronic fear. Psychologically, the infant is not only absolutely dependent upon but also absolutely identified with its parent. In the beginning, "I and My Parent Are One" describes the infant's emotional reality. Physical birth has taken place, but emotional birth is a long journey beginning sometime around the fifth month and, in some respects, lasting a lifetime. The infant and young child actually go through several phases of separation from the parent. Perhaps the most tumultuous phase occurs at about age two-and-a-half, hence the old pejorative label, "the terrible twos." A more accurate and, I think, more fair label might be "the terrifying twos." What's so frightening about being two? It's frightening because it marks a time of separation from parents. Two-year-olds are beginning to discover their own will. A favorite word at this age is "No!" Toddlers love this word. My son's favorite book when he was two was *The Baby Blue Cat Who Said No,* and he would chime in with a resounding no of his own every time the little cat in the story said "No!" to its mother.

This very favorite word is also frightening because perhaps more than any other word it represents separation from the parent. It says, I'm beginning to become my own person now. I have my own body to control and my own will and my own life to live. Notice the "my" word, second only to "no" in importance, but also scary because it also reveals one's solitariness.

"Good enough" parenting means knowing how to respond to the child's dual needs for freedom to experiment and defy authority (my wife's bumper sticker was evidence she didn't get to do enough of this—to take ownership of her things and her self and yet be mindful of her opposite need for reassurance, succor, and support). The young child is teetering precariously on that borderline between absolute dependence and relative freedom. And with this phase come wild swings in mood. A litmus test for how secure one is as a person may be in how well one is able to handle living with a two-year-old, whether it be an actual child or an adult whose emotional development was arrested somewhere around that age, which is not an uncommon thing!

To help make the transition, the young child develops transitional attachments to transitional objects, such as teddy bears, security blankets, thumbs, or persons other than Mom or Dad. These transitional objects serve two purposes. First, they are emotional substitutes for parents. Second, they lessen the importance of a parent's actual presence. Because of them, we do not have to have Mom and Dad with us at all times in order to feel secure. The doll or teddy bear taken to bed at night can be a very important companion in helping the young child face that loneliest of endeavors, falling asleep.[4]

Too often, a toddler's defiant Nos, possessiveness, and experiments with freedom are met with either overindulgence or with harshly judgmental reactions. Too often, parents who are themselves insecure are unable to strike that important balance between trusting permissiveness and firm boundary-setting that provides the secure environment for making transitions which the child so desperately needs.

Overdependence and Counterdependence   If our parents are too solicitous, anxious, or punitive, we have a really hard time making the transition from absolute dependence to relative autonomy. Insecure parenting in this phase can lead to one of two unhealthy expressions of our dependency strivings in adult life.

Too much hovering or too much distance or disapproval can lead us to become overdependent. We may never outgrow our need for transitional objects. Like Linus, we cling to one security blanket or another. Or we become parasites of other people. In adult life this overdependence can take the form of alcohol addiction or of codependence in a sick relationship.

On the other hand, we may react, as Mary did, by becoming counterdependent. Counterdependence, unlike genuine autonomy, is really a frantic effort not to need. The counterdependent individual is constantly having to fight against dependency yearnings. Most of us have problems with one or the other of these two negative expressions of dependency. We may even alternate between overdependence and counterdependence in different situations, although one expression tends to dominate and to determine our basic character. Either approach reveals a fundamentally frightened and insecure person.

People Who Hate People

Changing that one word "need" to "hate" ruins the lyrics of a lovely song. Streisand would probably never have hit the charts with a song about hate, but hate is also a song humanity sings. It is not the only song, nor does it always succeed in drowning out songs of love. The fact remains, however, that as human beings we experience and express powerful negative emotions: hate, guilt, and fear.

The Dual Risks of Love and Hate Childhood is an era of tremendous ambivalence. Adulthood is also, but the ambivalence of hate and love in childhood can be excruciating, particularly if the interpersonal environment is unsafe. Both loving and hating can be dangerous in an undependable emotional world.

The child who experiences frustration of need, be it need for food or emotional nurture, begins to feel ambivalent toward parents or other caregivers. While continuing to need them, he or she simultaneously begins to feel aggressive impulses toward them. "I hate you, Daddy!" such a child may blurt out in a moment of great frustration. If such intense anger is met with intolerance by an insecure father, the child is in a real bind. The human environment has become "bad," in the sense that it is hostile to the child's own budding capacity for hostility. As psychoanalyst Harry Guntrip puts it,

> When a child finds himself in a "bad" human environment, hostile and impinging, tantalizing and unsatisfying, or neglectful and deserting, he is in a serious predicament. How can he keep himself in being, let alone develop a personality in such a medium? What are his alternatives?[5]

The child really faces only two alternatives: to launch a protest and struggle angrily to improve his or her lot or to take flight mentally from this unsatisfactory interpersonal world and avoid any provocation to hate his or her parents by ceasing to feel anything. In both instances, the child employs a nifty psychological defense: bad or frustrating parental actions are internalized and repressed into the unconscious. This way, in conscious everyday life, the child can be aware of the parents as good. The world is not such an awful place after all.[6] The problem with this defense is that it leaves the "bad" inside the child and, later, inside the adult. This leads to low self-esteem. It also requires that the individual do something to get rid of the "bad" that is inside. Often what he or she does is to project it onto someone else. Projection is a psychological defense in which we get rid of our badness by attributing it to someone else. This can wreak havoc in important relationships—in a marriage, for instance—where frustrations of need and feelings of hate surface. Then you have two people, needing each other desperately but simultaneously hating and projecting their internal "bad" onto each other.

Feeling hostility toward a person we need can be dangerous. Expressing that hostility, to our parent, our mate, or our boss, can be a terrifying thing. Mary learned this early when her tantrums were doused with cold showers, her mother threatened to leave her, and her father threatened to disown her when she asserted her own will. It is little wonder that she spent the rest of her life bottling her hate and redirecting it to her "bad self." Many of us have faced similar dire consequences when we became angry at someone whose love we needed.

But there is an even greater risk than hating the one you love.

That greater risk is loving the one you love. What is risky about loving? The risk is that your love may be rejected, ignored, denied. If you are not received by the object of your love, you may feel as though your love went careening over a cliff to be dashed on the rocks below—and you with it.

Children are capable not only of great hate for their parents but tremendous feelings of love as well. I'm not talking about adaptively pleasing parents. I'm speaking of profound, spontaneous feelings of affection for their parents. Sometimes this love is expressed on the heels of hate. This is the child's way of making amends with Mother or Father and of being reassured that the hate has not ruined anything. Take, for example, the toddler who, earlier in the day, defiantly disobeyed his mother and then later picks some pretty yellow-flowered weeds with dear old Mom in mind. He presents his bouquet with a smile to which she, having not forgiven him, screams, "Get those nasty things out of here, you little brat!" Such a moment is singularly devastating. The child has risked love and attempted a rapprochement with the one he loves and needs most. What do you suppose he learns about love on such an occasion? Or the teenage girl who compliments her father on how nice he looks as he leaves for work and he, being preoccupied with his day's agenda, simply doesn't hear her. What does she learn about love? That it is risky business.

Achieving security with regard to our powerful feelings of love and hate involves acceptance of our own ambiguity. We must learn to become tolerant and understanding of our own hating, even when others are not. We need to reestablish a relationship to our own true self who loves, so that when our love is not received as we want we are not devastated and do not flee all relationships. How are we to achieve this? It is not easy because we erect massive defenses we are reluctant to abandon. These defenses promise security, but they actually fail us. They are substitutes for the real thing, for the personality ingredient that makes for true security. These defenses will be discussed more fully in chapter 3.

Guilt and Badness In addition to the powerful feelings of love and rage, the child—and, later, the adult—also has to deal with two other powerful states of mind, guilt and what I call a sense of "basic badness." I do not automatically regard guilt as something to be abolished. There are two reasons for this. First, real guilt can be a very constructive emotion, one that reveals maturity in the individual who is guilty. Real guilt arises in us when we have actually violated a moral code or done something to hurt someone else. The great thing about real guilt is that it has a motivating power. We are incited to do something to right the wrong we have done, to make amends, to confess and repent of our sins, and, we hope, to be forgiven and to forgive ourselves.

A second reason I do not try to abolish guilt is that some persons cling to it tenaciously, indicating that to relinquish their guilt at this moment would be very threatening for them. The guilt needs to be given up eventually, but it serves a vital function: it defends against something worse. If I am guilty, I am in a state of conditional badness. This means that, had I thought, willed, or acted rightly, I would have been good. The possibility of conceiving of oneself as good is still within reach if one is guilty.

Some people hold fast to their guilt precisely because it protects them from that something worse, a sense of *un*conditional badness. Remember, one of our earliest defenses against an undependable, rejecting interpersonal environment is to internalize it and send it down into the unconscious. What was outside is now inside. This psychological maneuver allows us to control "the bad" by keeping it out of sight, out of our awareness. But it comes back to haunt us. Now that it is inside, we are left feeling that it is we who are bad, unconditionally so. Staying guilty all the time helps us to ward off these utterly unbearable feelings of abject badness. Better to be guilty than pervasively bad.

Mary worked out her guilt in a religious context. But having done nothing morally terrible since her first religious experience on LSD, she was hard pressed to maintain a level of guilt. She was scrupulous at keeping the rules of her new ascetic religion. Still, she reassured herself she must have done something wrong. Repeatedly in therapy, she asked the question, "What did I do to deserve my childhood misery?" This question constituted her defense in the first phase of psychotherapy. Though not outright guilt, it was at least a striving toward guilt. Yet she could never identify an actual moral infraction on her part and was left with a sense of unconditional badness pressing on her consciousness.

Mary had a disturbing dream that captured perfectly her internal situation. She dreamed she was back at the divorce ranch in Nevada and received a notification in the mail of a two-thousand-dollar debt to various creditors. In utter dismay she told her mother about it, and her mother (in the dream) suggested she hire a lawyer.

In this dream Mary felt like a character in a Kafka novel, strangely haunted by a nagging but vague sense of culpability. As we discussed the dream, it became apparent that the two thousand dollars represented the enormous burden of indebtedness she felt toward her parents. Her very existence was a burden to her father, a drain on his artistic creativity. The debt might have been forgiven had she been a son, rather than a daughter. Also, Mary still felt guiltily tied to her mother. She once said that, even if it were possible for her to have a happy life, she couldn't do it because it would be so unfair to her mother, who had never known happiness.

Mary linked the number 2,000 and the lawyer with the figure of Christ. Christ would be her attorney, Christ who had canceled humanity's indebtedness. This image gave her courage, yet it also conjured up the idea of grace, which was still a foreign concept and not a little threatening to her. Things got worse before they got better. She continued to weave a thread of guilt through her internal system, but still the basic badness leaked through. Even a sense of basic badness was preferable to something still worse, a state of total weakness and raw fear.

Ego Weakness and Fear "The primary drive in every human being," says Harry Guntrip, "is to become a 'person,' to achieve a solid ego formation, to develop a personality in order to live."[7] This can only be achieved in the medium of personal relationships. In other words, we need the help of healthy relationships in order to actually become a person ourselves. "There are no fears worse or deeper," Guntrip says, "than those which arise out of having to cope with life when one feels that one is just not a real person, that one's ego is basically weak, perhaps that one is hardly an ego at all."[8]

Most of us, at one time or another, have felt this fear. Under conditions of prolonged or severe stress, even the strongest of us may cave in, feeling like a feeble, anemic child. Or we may feel empty inside, like a hollow shell of ourselves. Grief can produce this feeling. When we lose someone or something important, we experience a deep fatigue. We're tired of life, and it takes every ounce of energy we have to keep ourselves in being.

For some people whose egos were permanently weakened by the vicissitudes of childhood, this physical and emotional state can be chronic and ongoing. Each day they have to grab themselves by the scruff of the neck and literally force themselves out the door into the world of work and people. If they are lucky or especially adept, they can hide their fragileness behind a competent public mask. But underneath, they live with the constant dread that their ego will fragment or evaporate into nothing. Mary felt like this much of the time. Being with people drained her totally. At age eleven, she had a recurring dream of driving along in a car and suddenly disintegrating, which expressed the panic that accompanied her ego weakness. She knew she was not ready for the demands of adult life, including dealing with the opposite sex, but life's clock was ticking and forcing her out of the nest into what she perceived as a complex, cold, cruel world that was just too big for her. That the nest she was leaving had itself been too cold and too cruel figured heavily in the existence of her ego weakness.

Fear is the emotional component of ego weakness. Fear is the deepest and most powerful emotion the ego experiences. The countless ways that people are on the defensive against one another suggests that our most all-encompassing fear is the fear of being or appearing weak. As pointed out in chapter 1, our American society, which idolizes self-reliance and rugged individualism, hates weakness. That is why it hates dependency. Historically, humankind has denied and abhorred its weakness. We simply deny it. "We have these mighty aggressive, sexual, and territorial instincts," we reassure ourselves. We rattle our sabers lest anyone accuse us of wimpishness. Better to be guilty than bad. Better to be bad, yet strong, than to be weak.

The ego is weakened when the true self locks itself in its interior hiding place, cut off from the rest of personality, and from the world. The true self is that pristine inner child that possesses our unique talent and our dynamic power. But it is weakened by retreating to that impervious inner sanctum, because our true self, in order to thrive, requires contact with the rest of our self and with the outer world of energizing relationships.

Mary had a dream during therapy in which she was a little girl back at the ranch. In the dream, she was racing feverishly around the house trying to shut and lock all the windows to keep out some unknown danger. In closing its windows to danger, the true self, isolated and unattached, inevitably closes out the possibility of deliverance. Instead of being the safe hiding place, my inner sanctuary becomes the headquarters of fear.

How does one overcome fear of the many dangers of attachment? How did Mary do it? How, in light of the risks of love and hate, the fact of guilt and basic badness, and, above all, in light of our bedrock weakness and fear, is a person to achieve an abiding sense of security in this life and in this world? These are challenging questions. I hope in the remainder of this book to provide some answers. Pointing in that direction, I will say now that it involves achieving something akin to a conviction, born of experience, of the dependability and fundamental trustworthiness of life in this world. This conviction must grow out of experience. How do we allow ourselves to experience this possibility? First, we have to become aware of the defenses we employ that actually prevent us from experiencing the love and reassurance we need. In becoming aware of them, we need to assess their value to us and make a decision about whether or not to keep them or let them go. That is our topic for the next chapter. Meanwhile, sing it again, Barbra!

Questions for Reflection

1. In what setting and with whom are you most likely to feel free to be your true self: At work? At home? Anywhere? With friends? Family? Work associates? No one? What kind of interpersonal dangers are apt to force you into your false self?

2. In what ways can you identify with Mary's struggle? How have you experienced rejection by the important people in your life? How did the experience of rejection affect your attitude about relationships in general?

3. What scares you the most about relationships? Are you typically counterdependent or overdependent in relationships? Which is riskier for you, loving or hating someone you need?

3

The High Cost of Defense

Because most of us do not develop or operate from a conviction that our interpersonal world is fully dependable and safe, we naturally feel a need to protect ourselves. We develop elaborate measures of defense. How else are we to achieve a sense of security? Who in this world could lead a "defenseless" life?

This chapter identifies and interprets some of the defenses we use to help us feel secure. This examination will show that these defenses actually fail to make us secure and may actually exaggerate our insecurity.

This litany of defenses is a short one and is by no means exhaustive. One could dedicate an entire book to the subject, and many have. While the defenses discussed here do involve intricate psychological mechanisms, I will avoid a highly technical approach. Rather, I will view these defenses as if they were personal policies resulting from basic attitudes about living and interacting. More often than not these basic attitudes and policies function at an unconscious level, outside our awareness. Rarely do they ascend to the level of a conscious conviction, as we saw in Mary's declaration, "I can leave any relationship and never feel anything." We are halfway to freedom when, like Mary, we do become conscious of our defenses. Then they can be examined for what they are. Then when those red-alert situations do arise, being conscious of our characteristic defensive patterns can lend wisdom and freedom to our defensive behavior. Ultimately, the more our personal security depends on something other than an elaborate but obsolete defense system, the more our energies will be freed up for creativity and real relationship. As our psychic economy benefits by the new energy resources available to it, we will come to know, perhaps for the first time, the meaning of joy.

Abandonment, Absorption, and Our Need for Control

As human beings, we are inveterate controllers. This is not an altogether bad thing. Civilization is the result of our impulse to control ourselves and the environment. But our need to control can reach excesses in both our interpersonal and our international relations.

You will recall from chapter 2 that our earliest defense against an unsafe interpersonal environment is to internalize the bad aspects and push them down into our unconscious so we can view our world as better than it is. This nifty bit of self-deception allows us to survive and to work on constructing our person. It outlives its usefulness, however, and, worse, along with our other defenses, actually skews our efforts to build our personal identity. Our very character comes to be built around our particular defenses! This original defense, instead of being abandoned when we grow to the point that we are less vulnerable to the pain inflicted by others, spawns an entire repertoire of new defenses. These new defenses, we are unconsciously convinced, will add to our security.

Famed American psychiatrist Harry Stack Sullivan even referred to these defenses as "security operations."[1] They are mechanisms that enable us to get along with and to feel secure with those we need. I prefer the term "defense" because it connotes the state of interpersonal warfare in which we so often find ourselves.

What are the battle lines in this interpersonal war? They tend to be drawn between two opposite threats present in most important relationships: the threat of abandonment, at one extreme, and the threat of absorption at the other. If someone is important to me, if his or her attitude toward me influences my own self-concept and my self-esteem, there are two dangers posed by being in relationship to this person. One is the threat of leaving me. He or she might die, become disgusted with me or just disinterested, or might abandon the true me by adopting a fixed, stereotypical image of me and relating to it rigidly,

leaving the real me disregarded and unknown. Emotional abandonment can take many forms. Likewise, the threat of absorption has many faces. Someone who is strong might overwhelm
me through the sheer weight of personality, overpower me by
force of will. His or her life agenda and worldview might eclipse
my own.

These dual threats are nothing to sneeze at in this business of
living and relating. They have great significance. All our problems with the ambivalence of love and hate, guilt and badness,
ego weakness and fear are encompassed in and get worked out
along this continuum between abandonment and absorption.
This occurs not only in marriage but in just about any relationship. Partners in a business experience the dual threats. What
if the other guy pulls out of the partnership? What if he over-
powers me on important decisions? Children feel the dual
threats with their parents, but the reverse may also be the case:
the child may rule the roost, with the parents mired in the
child's emotions and issues. On the flip side, mothers and fathers
may resist a child's growing up because of the underlying threat
of abandonment by this child upon whom they have emotionally
come to depend.

But it is in the battle of the sexes that the abandonment/
absorption theme appears in its sharpest contrast. This theme
is worked out in a myriad of ways during marriage counseling.
The partners tend to camp out at opposite ends of the continuum, one fearing absorption, the other sensitive to any hint
of abandonment, but the positions are easily exchanged, often
depending on the marital issue at stake.

Defenses Against Absorption

Persons who fear absorption in a relationship have usually
had experiences in childhood of being impinged on by others.
They experienced attachments as dangerous in a variety of ways
such as smothering, stifling, suffocating, or manipulating. They
may never have had adequate privacy. Their personal boundaries were violated. I have seen numerous adolescents whose
parents were busy invading their privacy, eavesdropping on
their telephone conversations, rifling through their drawers for

evidence of this misdemeanor or that. Earlier, they may have been burdened by exaggerated parental expectations, which were embellished and translated internally into even higher self-expectations. More subtly, they may have felt themselves being overdetermined by their parents' version of who they were, who they ought to be. They felt pressured to become their false self. Their true self never had room to breathe.

Often the absorption-fearing person becomes the abandoner in relationships. He or she is usually counterdependent, which means keeping those powerful dependency yearnings under tight rein. Closeness, for this person, equals the risk of being swallowed up by another's need or personality. He or she therefore employs an array of defenses designed to keep distance.

Absolutizing Thought and Language

One of the hallmarks of maturity is the capacity to tolerate ambivalence in oneself and ambiguity in the world. Personal security does not hinge on the world's being cut-and-dried. But many people, especially those who experienced the emotional deprivation and overstimulation that accompanies absorption, insist on reducing the world to these unambiguous categories. They become absolutizers.

If, in their being absorbed by their omnipresent parents, these persons experienced an unpredictable alternation between judgmentalism and commendation, they come to adulthood terribly confused about what elicits punitive or affirmative responses. They see no rhyme or reason to human interaction. Naturally, they want things to be nailed down. They are apt to gravitate toward absolutizing or moralizing religious groups, groups that make it clear what is expected of their members. Not surprisingly, therefore, they often cover themselves in the false security blanket of religious absolutism described in chapter 1.

Absolutizers reveal the dual tendencies to exaggerate and to oversimplify situations in life. In a brilliant essay on what he calls the "absolutizing instinct," Father William Lynch says of the tendency to exaggerate, "The good becomes the tremendously good, the evil becomes the absolutely evil, the grey becomes the black or white, the complicated, because it is difficult to handle, becomes in desperation the completely simple."[2] Of this latter point, the tendency to oversimplify, he goes on to say:

> One of the most common of all [forms of absolutizing], to which we are all subject to some degree, is the human tendency to expect a single, simple way of thinking in any human situation. One may call this the desire for some absolute in the situation. If we love, we think that we should have no negative feelings. If we are angry, we tend to fear that love cannot coexist with the anger. In brief, we fear that if we hate we do not love. We want to be in the presence of one feeling, one thought.[3]

Absolutizing is favored by the absorption-anxious individual precisely because it helps to establish distance. Absolutizers are utopian. They will settle for nothing less than a perfect situation, so they do not have to invest themselves in any real situation, one with imperfections. Likewise, if they can detect imperfection in someone else and reduce it to a simple stereotype, whenever they are tempted to become involved, they can flourish their absolutes and justify pulling back.

This absolutizing is most damaging when it is employed against a family member. Parents use it when their children reach adolescence and begin to gain power by virtue of their budding adult minds, their physical growth, their maturing voices imploring for—even demanding—freedom. A mother may feel almost as vulnerable to absorption by an adolescent child as she did to her own domineering mother. Now, as an adult, it is her turn to domineer, and she can do this if she stereotypes her child as bad. Insecure fathers also give in to this temptation.

Husbands and wives, of course, employ this technique all the time. Either they relate to their own projected or cast-off characteristics now superimposed on the other or they relate to their mate as if he or she were someone from their past. In all this they absolutize, exaggerating the other's flaws and drawing sweeping conclusions about their mate based on the flimsiest of evidence. Partners in a marriage may even develop their own absolutizing language, and certain choice words can trigger a fight in a minute. Absolutizing language in a marriage quarrel can be quite inflammatory. The couple find themselves repeating the same old phrases, involved in the same old weary battles, so wedded to their defenses they are stuck, like a marital broken record.

Absolutizing language, to be destructive, does not even have to be vituperative. Some couples draw upon otherwise innocuous words. When Sherry and Fred came for marriage counseling, feeling insecure in their marriage, Sherry claimed that Fred was always undependable, that she was weary of his demands and of playing the role of his mother. She was afraid of being absorbed by this dependent man upon whom she could never count for understanding or support. Fred, on the other hand, complained that his wife was domineering and always cold and that he could never count on her for consistent love and affection. Notice the use of the absolutes "always" and "never." Both Sherry and Fred had had emotionally traumatic childhoods. Each vacillated between the two poles of absorption fear and abandonment fear, though Sherry tended to settle at the absorption end, while Fred was more threatened by abandonment. Both had developed defective defenses for guaranteeing security in relationship. They both brought into their marriage a tremendous need for a partner who would provide the emotional security they had seldom known. However, because of the extremity of their respective needs for love from the other and their basic defensive policies, they overwhelmed and intimidated each other.

One of the defenses they shared in common was their use of absolutizing language. By saying "always" and "never" to stereotype the other, they each gained a measure of control and protection against crushing disappointment. In other words, "Since I will settle for nothing less than a perfect response from you, something I never really expect anyway, I'll not be disappointed when you let me down. And I'll be entitled to feel angry with you and to disengage myself from you." Unfortunately, this automatic defensive policy of reducing the other to one dimension also prevented them from achieving the close marital bond they desired.

Most of us have been the victim at one time or another of someone else's predetermined and fixed notion of who we are and what we are about. This can be a terribly frustrating and distancing thing. Most of us, like Sherry and Fred, have been guilty of employing this defense. Sometimes it is so automatic that we are on a paranoid roll before we know it and this person we need has suddenly become the devil incarnate. We begin to believe our own propaganda, which denies any complexity to our partner's character, and soon we are in a cold war, shadow boxing with grotesque distortions of ourselves and our significant others, preparing for an all-out war that should never have started in the first place. Are we really more secure as a result of our absolutizing defense?

Standing Outside Space and Time

Closely related to the absolutizing defense is what I call "standing outside space and time." Now, of course, no one can really pull this off, not even an Einstein! But you might be surprised how many people attempt to find a place just outside the city limits of the known universe in which to dwell. People ridden with absorption anxiety are the most likely to adopt this clever defense. They locate themselves in an ethereal fantasy land, where they can avoid the demands of relationships and, equally important, can postpone decisions regarding those relationships indefinitely.

Again, these persons chafe at constraints on their freedom. Hating their finitude, they strive for absolute freedom. They want to be everywhere at the same time. Some attempt to keep themselves outside of time by staying involved with two romantic partners, their spouse and an extramarital other. Bill, for example, left his wife of twenty-five years, married and honeymooned with his paramour of several years, then immediately had that marriage annulled and returned hastily to his first wife. Even then, however, he could not give up his passion for the other woman. Both women were fed up with his wavering and vacillation. Both wanted him to make up his mind. Naturally, they each wanted a commitment. Bill was a tormented and divided soul. "Torn Between Two Lovers" could have been his theme song. He felt foolish, but a part of him secretly enjoyed breaking society's rules.

Bill had become aware of his finitude at an early age. Born with a skeletal birth defect, he was quite incapacitated as a young child and his life hung in the balance several times. He recalls having great ambivalence toward his hovering, solicitous mother, on the one hand drawing comfort from her ministrations, on the other resenting being treated differently from his strong, manly brothers. One of those brothers drowned and Bill was forever saddled with survivor's guilt. Why hadn't he, "the cripple," been the one to die? Bill had tremendous drive and, through sheer perseverance, pulled himself up and forged ahead, becoming a successful professional. But always there was that underlying feeling of insecurity and that dim, haunting awareness of his mortality and fragility. Every time he achieved financial security, he would overspend his budget and put himself at destitution's door. Then he'd pull himself out of the fiscal fire in some flamboyant fashion, as if compulsively repeating his childhood heroism.

Bill was also an absolutizer. His every crisis, his every action, his every feeling was writ large or painted in sweeping swaths of red across his life's canvas. Melodrama was his way of keeping himself in being, as if to remind himself that his life was a truly tragic and therefore momentous event. Thus he denied his own decay and kicked back death.

Bill married his childhood sweetheart but could not commit to his wife completely lest he become absorbed by her domesticity, thus revealing an ambivalence similar to that he had felt toward his mother. He needed a secret life that was his own, so he became a kind of Don Juan version of Walter Mitty. At age forty-five, he entered therapy with life's clock pounding in his ears like Big Ben.

Bill's romantic dilemma was really his defensive cover for a deeper problem. His fear of absorption by a woman was really symbolic of his deeper fear of being finite, engulfed in space and time. Making a decision to keep a commitment was tantamount in his mind to entering the real world of real time where, sooner or later, he would die. By forever living torn between two women, he kept his options open. He could continue to aspire to absolute freedom and to a kind of immortality now.[4] But standing outside of time and space requires an inordinate amount of energy. Bill was drained by his inner conflict. His defense against absorption was wearing him out. After all, at age forty-five, one has only so much energy to spare for such things.

How, then, can we find security in the thick of real life? I turned forty while writing this chapter and can easily identify with Bill's desire to stand outside space and time. While my wife swears I'm going deaf because I don't hear her (my altogether creative defense against absorption!), I can still hear that relentless ticking of life's clock. I fantasize about all kinds of other lives I might be living. Then I say to myself, "No, these are my numbered days. This is the day the Lord hath made. Think I'll give it my best shot." Doing so, however, requires that I lay aside a defense I am tempted to use again and again. I must contend with that grandiose and escapist part of me that wants to be everywhere at the same time.

Faultfinding, Perfectionism, and Self-righteousness

While many of us use distancing defenses that move us horizontally away from those who threaten to absorb us, there are also some vertical maneuvers that enable us to achieve the desired distance. Most of these are designed to protect our self-esteem. Given our human tendency to become identified with someone important to us, there is always the risk that the other's failures will reflect badly on us, or even that something about the other will stir up feelings of our own badness. Whenever we come within the other's sphere of influence, we have to be on guard.

Faultfinding is one such vertical defense. The faultfinder knows that the best defense is a good offense, which is to say that, for all their unsolicited criticalness, faultfinders are, deep down, defending themselves against overwhelming assaults to their esteem. Having been cornered by the overbearing criticism of their original significant others, that criticism, now internalized, has become an ongoing self-criticism at some subliminal level. In other words, despite their ability to zero in on another's flaws, they remain, at some level, their own worst critic. When all is said and done, faultfinders are really harder on themselves than on anyone else.

The problem is that by hiding behind a barrage of indictments against those around them, faultfinders are inaccessible to help. In the first place, they seldom recognize that what they are doing is defending themselves. They are convinced they are merely pointing out the truth about others. If you don't like it, too bad; it's your problem! In the second place, they are often quite perceptive in their criticism of others. Having been the object of criticism early on, faultfinders know how to sniff out another's weaknesses. Feeling insecure themselves, they have become adept at scouting out the Achilles' heels of others. They often succeed at hooking the other person's self-doubt, so they don't have to come to terms with their own. They remain "one up" in most of their relationships.

Perfectionism is a similar defense. Perfectionists want their world to be just so. They relate more intensely to something inside their own head, their own ideal of perfection, than to people. Whereas faultfinders zero in on the other guy's faults, perfectionists hold everybody accountable, including most of all themselves, to a rigorous standard of human excellence. The ideologies may vary, but the idealism remains the common link between perfectionists. It is an idealism, however, that isolates them and sets them apart from their significant others. Consider, for example, the mother in *Ordinary People.* Her uncompromisingly Spartan approach to life sets her above her son, who is struggling not only with horrible survivor's guilt, following his brother's drowning, but with his mother's contempt for his suicidal weakness. Her perfectionism renders her cold, stiff, and unsympathetic as a mother. She clings to her hard and haughty social Darwinism as a defense against her own overwhelming sorrow. This defense also permits her to project her own internal bad (her own weakness and the dread fact that she lives in a world where a mother can lose her child) onto her remaining son.[5]

Closely related to faultfinding and perfectionism is the defense of self-righteousness. The self-righteous usually employ the faultfinding defense but they go a step farther or, actually, a step higher. They also tend to be absolutizers. Using their own moral or religious hierarchy of values, and sitting upon some throne of objectivity, they judge the world around them. Again, underneath it all they feel bad about themselves. Their self-righteousness defends them against overwhelming self-criticism, even self-loathing. It enables them to expel the bad that is inside onto the world of pinkos, Commies, radicals, reprobates, liberals, conservatives, geeks, nerds, derelicts, hypocrites, and other "sinners" in the outside world. On a more intimate plane, they are always just a moral cut above their spouse, their children, their co-workers, and even the friends who stick by them. They regulate their self-esteem, ward off shame, and avoid engulfment in a grimy, sleazy, interpersonal world by way of this vertical defense. In their minds they become superior to those they need.

Defenses Against Abandonment

Persons who fear abandonment, and who build their personalities upon defenses against this dread, usually had the experience in childhood of being emotionally forsaken. They viewed attachment as dangerous because it was tenuous, ephemeral, slippery, seductive, rejecting, unpredictable, and unreliable. They never felt secure in the love and approval of those whose love and approval they needed most. They were often left to their own devices too early in life. As children they lived with too much loneliness, in some cases interspersed with periods of intense overstimulation in the form of parental judgment, prying, or accusation. But these interruptions of loneliness were as unpredictable as their cessation was inevitable. The child could not count on consistently holding the interest of the parent.

Those who fear abandonment are constantly in search of reassurance, love, and approval in their relationships. They glue themselves to people. They may become abandoners, but more often they are the clinging vine in the relationship. They don't know how to leave a relationship or to draw the line with someone on matters important to them. They hate arguments, although they frequently find themselves arguing. They hate separation of any kind and will work a relationship to death. Their great fear is of being rejected by those they need, and abandonment can assume many forms for them. Even constructive criticism can be their undoing, so vulnerable is their self-esteem to another person's opinion. Their defenses differ from those whose overriding fear is of absorption. As you would expect, the defenses of an abandonment-fearing person are designed to eliminate distance and separation.

Chameleon and "Cry Uncle"

Those who fear abandonment may protect themselves by becoming social chameleons. They adapt themselves to others. They can always blend in. They seldom show their own true colors because doing so might lead to rejection. This defense should not be confused with what I call "empathic identification," which is a strength. We see this in persons who, in the interest of communication and understanding, eliminate unnecessary barriers by adopting the accent and accepting the worldview of the person to whom they are relating. In contrast, persons employing the chameleon defense are so busy being self-conscious, preoccupied with their own status or with how they are perceived by others, they never really tune in to another to find out whether that person is also anxious. They would be astounded to discover that someone else in a given social situation was also running scared!

Sara, a talented writer who wound up editing other authors' works but never managed to finish her own masterpiece, was a chameleon. She feared completing it because, in doing so, she would open herself to criticism and possible rejection. She would also find herself standing out there alone, isolated and exposed, on her own two little feet in a competitive literary world.

Closely related is the defense of crying uncle. Those who use this defense avoid abandonment, condemnation, and rejection by giving up too quickly. They are like the lower-echelon wolf in the pack who, in order not to threaten or offend his superior, presents his own jugular in an act of submission. Hating conflict because of the potential for abandonment, they raise the white flag of surrender before the battle begins, despite the fact that they may possess superior strength, like the natural woman athlete who chokes, blowing a big lead in the tennis match she's practiced for over the past three months because she winds up playing her best friend in the finals.

Ever since a life-threatening stroke at nineteen, Paul found that he frequently sabotaged his own success through chronic anxiety and scrupulousness. He burned up so much psychic energy worrying over what might go wrong that he was less effective in his career than his talent implied. Although resilient in his heroic climb out of the jaws of death, there was an underlying cynicism, a conviction that this unsafe world would do him in at a moment's notice. The worry kept him from being productive and, consequently, from ever being ambushed while riding high. It was as if he carried a white flag on him permanently, ready to surrender. This defended him against being blindsided and against feeling paralyzed by the thought of his own sudden death separating him from his wife and children. Once he began to come to terms with his conviction about the nature of the world, he relinquished his defense and began to relax and enjoy the present and be more productive in his career.

Loaning Love

Another defense of those who dread being left is that of loaning love rather than giving it freely. In the first place, these persons seldom received love as a free gift. They had to earn it. Being accepted was always conditional on performing up to the expectations of others. Love was experienced as something borrowed that always had to be paid back, usually with interest. Consequently, in their adult relationships, these persons operate on the same budgetary principle of love.

This approach to relationships usually involves the notion that love is quantifiable and limited. The person who loves three others must be careful to parcel this love out in equal portions, since it is a finite amount. Often, these individuals were intense rivals for affection with their siblings. They may have actually been cheated by their parents' favoritism toward one child over another.

Those who make loans of love at high interest rates do so as a defense against abandonment or rejection. If they were not their parents' favorite, they may attempt to find that special role with their mate, their child, their pastor, their boss, or their friend. In therapy, they seek to be the special favorite, often resenting other patients and incredulous that the therapist can actually care about all those people without running low on therapeutic love.

Loaners of love create debtors of persons they need, thereby binding them almost as indentured servants. As a way to control abandonment fear, they go out of their way to do for others, spending money, running errands, sending cards, leaving love notes around the house, sponsoring educational and other pursuits. They go the extra mile every chance they get, but always with the hidden motive of piling up a large interpersonal bank note with the other's name on it. Whenever the other begins to manifest independence in a threatening way, they call in the note. Ironically, this strategy for avoiding abandonment often disposes those they need, weary of always being debtors, actually to pull away.

Self-effacement and Psychic Merger

The abandonment-anxious person puts a premium on the response of others. He or she is other-directed, finding salvation in others. Other people hold the key to self-acceptance and esteem. Some individuals utilize a self-effacing defense against abandonment. This defense determines their entire character. They become compliant and self-deprecating in most of their important relationships. They frequently put themselves down, a ploy designed to invite compliments and reassurances from others, but which they can never accept or internalize. They remain inferior to others, always in a one-down position.

Karen Horney, who writes about the self-effacing solution to inner conflict, says of these persons as children:

> After some years, in which the wish to rebel struggled in the child's heart with his need for affection, he suppressed his hostility, relinquished the fighting spirit, and the need for affection won out. Temper tantrums stopped and he became compliant, learned to like everybody and to lean with a helpless admiration on those whom he feared the most.[6]

Self-effacing individuals may actually possess tremendous talent and intellect. But they desperately fear having their superiority exposed. Why? Because that is to risk being set apart. There is a tendency toward self-deprecation among those counselees who are extraordinarily gifted. Their gift is often experienced by them as a double burden. First, they fear they may never live up to the expectations implicit in their giftedness. Second, their giftedness sets them apart from their peers in most uncomfortable ways, the major exception in our culture being athletic endowment. Intellectual prowess and aesthetic talent can evoke derision and social exile, particularly among adolescents. Who wants to be labeled a geek or a nerd?

Self-effacing individuals hide their anger and their personal power lest they risk alienating someone they need. Women in our culture incur an added pressure to hide their power, lest they threaten and drive away their men. Amanda, at forty an accomplished high school mathematics teacher, admitted to a kind of "inverse cheating" on exams in high school in order to lower her grade point average to avoid standing out in the crowd. Her mother had admonished her that boys wouldn't want to date her if she were too smart. When I saw her for psychotherapy, Amanda was still struggling with a conflict between career goals and romantic needs. Having been twice divorced after marriages to insecure and less talented men (I once made the mistake of referring to one of them as a loser and she rallied to his defense!), she was trying hard to make herself more appealing to men. One part of her had fantasized about going to medical school, but a stronger pressure was finally to succeed at love and marriage.

Amanda berated herself for lacking some unknown but important feminine quality that might lure a man. When her last love turned out to be gay, she agonized over whether there was something really wrong with her that she attracted men who could not really commit to her. In addition to self-effacement, Amanda employed another defense against abandonment, that of psychic merger with others. She longed for that perfect union, that romantic oneness where boundaries blur and hearts are welded together. As a single mother of two, Amanda wearied, as do many of us, of the burden of her own individuality. And the added burden of her considerable unexpressed potential left her excruciatingly alone. She wanted to melt into somebody else, to be taken hold of and determined. She wanted to experience the ecstasy of passionate self-surrender. She felt this to be her true vocation and even recalled a powerful dream in early childhood about a dark handsome man she would someday marry. But Mr. Right never appeared. She tried to force the feeling with nearly every man she dated. She would begin every relationship by idealizing the man and putting herself down. Soon, however, it became apparent to her that she was simply trying too hard. She began to question her own policy of self-deprecation and her search for the perfect union. Eventually, Amanda was able to let go of her self-effacing defense, to own her giftedness without apology, and to abandon the notion that her life would be forever incomplete unless she was psychically glued to some man. She was accepted in medical school at age forty-three. How did she manage to free herself from her self-effacing defense and her merger mania? The transformation involved the recovery of her true self, which had been lost under the weight of her feminine socialization. It also involved a recovery of an orienting faith, which permitted her to view this life and God's world as replenishing rather than as depriving of love.

Leaving Before You Are Left

A final defense against abandonment is a policy of leaving before you are left. An example is the person who, fearing rejection to the extreme, backs away from a relationship before his or her weaknesses become manifest. I well remember times in college when I would start to call a girl for a date but would hang up the phone before I finished dialing because my mouth was so dry and I was breathing so hard I feared I couldn't speak. There was one very attractive girl I would call at the last minute on Friday night for a date on Saturday, knowing full well she would already have plans. This young woman had a wonderfully gracious way of letting me down easy, making it seem as though she were really disappointed she couldn't go out with me. I got in the habit of calling her several Friday nights in a row just so I could get the ego boost that came with her every turndown. Stupid me; I learned years later that she had actually wanted to go out with me and naturally had interpreted my eleventh-hour invitations as evidence of supreme arrogance on my part. Little did she know—little did I know at that stage—that I was defending against rejection by leaving before I was left.

Those who employ this defense are usually only bluffing. It is absorption-anxious persons who are serious about leaving their significant others. Abandonment-anxious individuals merely want the partner to think this is the case. Emily threatened divorce precisely when she was uncertain about whether her husband loved her or approved of her. She was mortified when he countered by calling her bluff—and his attorney!

In psychotherapy, persons with high abandonment anxiety will start to miss their appointments and may even pull out of therapy prematurely. Because they know themselves to be needy and dependent, they fear their therapist will tire of them. Mary asked me repeatedly if I was growing weary of her lack of progress. Deep down, she feared not only being devoured by me, engulfed, but, even worse, she feared she might devour me with her neediness. Interestingly, she would eat less and less each day before a counseling session and then, after our session, would go home and feast on junk food. It was as if she was telling herself not to need, not to be hungry, lest she destroy or drive away or be abandoned by me because her need was too great. She defended herself against abandonment by leaving before she was left.

We have seen in this chapter how, in light of our experience of human interpersonal life as dangerous and potentially hurtful, we develop defenses we believe will protect us from further harm. These defenses are policies of interaction with others arising from our deep conviction that life is depriving, painful, and undependable. We experience our basic human dependency, from birth forward, as problematic, as posing a great dilemma.

All of us find ourselves somewhere on the absorption/abandonment continuum in life, and we are seldom at ease with ourselves or with others at any point on that continuum. We all vary in our defenses along this continuum, and we fluctuate in our use of defenses designed either to bind others to us or to keep them at arm's length. In my case, I tend to use defenses against abandonment in my relations with men and defenses against absorption in my relations with women. Usually our defenses only worsen our situation, our dilemma of both needing others and dreading others. Keeping ourselves defended and protected requires so much psychic energy that our creative juices are depleted.

Is it possible to live life without these defenses? I believe it is! Ultimately, by relinquishing our defenses we will open ourselves to the healing resources that make life not merely livable but exciting, fulfilling, and enjoyable. But we are not apt to tear down our walls of defense until we are convinced that to do so will not utterly destroy us. Some basic attitude changes, based on new perspectives on life experiences, will necessarily precede the laying down of arms and seeking peace with the world.

Questions for Reflection

1. Which type of anxiety governs your relationships with other people, absorption or abandonment? Given your life experience, why do you think you operate from your particular end of the absorption/abandonment continuum?

2. Take inventory of your own defense system. List on a piece of paper the defenses from this chapter that you employ. Try to be honest with yourself. Add any other defenses you use that are not mentioned in the chapter. Which defenses are your favorites? Which ones are obsolete or counterproductive?

3. Next to each defense you listed, write the name of someone with whom you are prone to use that particular defense. How do your children, your spouse, your friends, or others close to you react to that particular defense? What defenses are they apt to use against you? Do your defenses really make you more secure?

4. What is the cost in interpersonal terms of your defense system? Does it cost you closeness, mutuality, openness, trust, or the satisfaction of needs in your relationships? What would it cost you to relinquish your defenses?

4

Opening the Way
to Security

What, then, are the initial steps involved in overcoming insecurity? These steps actually involve profound changes in perspective and attitude. Having read this far, you have already begun to acknowledge that insecurity is a problem for you and that you have built up a costly arsenal of defenses to deal with it. While it may not seem like much, that very admission is a real beginning toward solving your insecurity problems. It is only a beginning, however. The rest involves some intense self-examination and the willingness to change. What follows in this chapter and the next two is a discussion of the changes which, if you will allow them to occur in you, can lead to the overcoming of insecurity.

Mastery: Doing Unto Life What Life Has Done Unto You

In chapter 2 we saw that the very first defense we employ is that of internalizing the bad that is outside. What was outside (rejecting, frustrating, untrustworthy, inadequate, or indifferent messages from a parent) is now inside, where we can manage it. After taking in the badness that is outside, we manage it by repressing it into our unconscious.

The problem, we found, is that the bad won't stay down there in our unconscious. It keeps popping up, pressing on our consciousness, influencing our everyday life and affecting how we feel about ourselves and about others. This is because a part of us is connected to that badness. "Bad me, bad world" becomes the deep unconscious basis of our self-identification. This identification leads to a deep conviction about life and love. The defenses described in the previous chapter are really the outgrowth of a basic conviction that, from an emotional survival standpoint, "I and the world in which I dwell are bad." It predisposes us to be defensive because it presupposes a bad world.

Far from being merely passively defensive, however, most of us launch an offensive program as well, one that seeks somehow to right the wrongs of our existence. We want to alter the situation in such a way that we win rather than lose the important emotional battles. We want to return the bad that is inside back to its origination point outside us, which usually entails relocating it in someone else. Ironically, we compulsively and repeatedly put ourselves in similar vulnerable emotional situations as a way to try to rectify the interpersonal injustices of the past and to get even with a world that hurt us when we were small and helpless. Freud appropriately called this human tendency the "repetition compulsion."[1] I think of it as a psychological law of the talon ("an eye for an eye and a tooth for a tooth," Matt. 5:38), at work in us unconsciously, a striving to do unto life what life has done unto us. It is as if now, in adulthood, I can master all the historic pain inside by setting up interpersonal situations identical to those in which I was hurt as a child. Only this time, I will prevail!

Repetition compulsion appears in relationships in many ways. A classic example is the man (or woman) who marries one alcoholic after another. Such a man needs to feel superior to his spouse and is determined to reform her. However, he may unwittingly sabotage her efforts at recovery because her recovery threatens his mode of mastering some past pain with his own domineering, alcoholic mother. Husbands and wives who find themselves fighting the same old weary verbal battles they have always fought—same song, three millionth verse—are stuck in their marital repetition compulsion, possessed of the futile conviction that sooner or later one of them will triumph over the other.

A major feature of growing toward maturity is making the unconscious conscious. When unconscious repetition compulsion is made conscious, the individual is freed up to master his or her pain and environment, with the benefit of reason and self-control. Ego psychologists refer to this as the "mastery

principle" that governs ego development.[2] The mastery principle refers to our conscious drive to grow up, to cope with the
tasks and difficulties that confront us at each stage of life, and
to get on with the business of living.

Conceived of as a means to an end, the human ego's striving
for mastery of emotions and environment is a natural and good
thing. Theologically speaking, it is precisely our capacity to
master God's world by our human reason and moral sensitivi-
ties that sets us apart from the other creatures in creation.
Humanity is given dominion and is instructed to subdue creation (Gen. 1:28). Civilization results from such mastery, as do
all the accomplishments of modern science. At the individual
level, our development as persons does depend on our success
at mastering the challenges we face during the various epochs
of development. My two-year-old son is currently fascinated
with language and intoxicated by his newfound word power. His
incessant chatter from daybreak to sundown—much of which
includes imperial pronouncements in the imperative mood such
as "Wake up, Daddy! I want to eat!"—is welcome evidence that
he is mastering communication skills at a developmentally ripe
moment.

At one level, psychotherapy itself can be viewed as an enterprise whose goal is to help a person convert blind repetition into
the conscious and intentional mastering of problems. Good
counseling strives to improve the mastery skills of persons.
When an individual who is struggling to cope with depression
from within and pressure from without enters psychotherapy,
that person mainly needs support and the psychic space that
therapy affords in order to recover the capacity to master the
situation. My wife, also a psychotherapist, has treated many
victims of rape and incest. Often, these persons are besieged by
recurring nightmares about the rape. Using art therapy, she
often has the victim draw a picture of the dream, and then
introduces the dramatic element of having the victim triumph
in some way over the rapist, even inflicting some harm to him.
This can be a tremendously liberating experience; a surprising
number report that they actually had the dream again but were
able to control the outcome as they had in the drawing. This is
ego mastery at its therapeutic best, where persons overcome

trauma and tragedy in the interest of life and growth. Victimization yields to personal empowerment.

Even so, the woman is still left to figure out the meaning of her life in a world where something as horrible as rape can occur. She must determine her prevailing attitude toward the opposite sex. Here is where mastery alone fails us. More often than not, the mastery principle leads to the defensiveness described in chapter 3. In order to master our insecurity in this menacing world of people, we must be wary, guarded, and vigilant against danger and threat. Based on the mastery principle, our defensive posture is supported by a deep conviction regarding the undependability of our interpersonal world and a policy of vengeance, "Do unto life (all our current and future significant others) what life has done unto us (all the wounds inflicted by parents and others)."

When applied to a given task, mastery has its place, but it fails us as an ultimate policy for achieving security in interpersonal relationships. If my interpersonal goal is to win or be the best, then mastery should be the operative motive. For example, in a competitive sport my security depends on my beating the other guy, not on my establishing a relationship with him. In fact, motivation to win is aided by the revenge factor present in sports rivalries. However, even in sports, the mastery principle never provides true security. It is only a matter of time before an unbeaten team meets its match. In our search for security, mastery ultimately fails us.

I remember the great insecurity I felt as a third-grader because of Carl, the big bully down the street. I could never pass Carl's house without trepidation. On my journeys home, he was often waiting in ambush to knock me down. One day, as I came wimpishly crying toward my own front door after one of Carl's beatings, the imposing figure of our housekeeper and adjunct mother, Charlie Mae, barred the door. She informed me that I could not come inside until I had gone back and dealt with Carl once and for all. I was to let Carl know in whatever way I was able to communicate that he had assaulted me for the last time. Gulping down my fear, I set my jaw in the direction of Carl's terrorist compound and prepared for the showdown. Sure enough, Carl was there waiting, and I told him in my most ferocious voice that from now on he was to leave me alone! As I predicted, he attacked. Only this time, less fearful of Carl than of Charlie Mae's wrath, I threw him to the ground, much to my surprise and to his total dismay. Carl never bothered me again. We had both learned a lesson, and I am forever grateful for Charlie Mae's firmness. Charlie Mae knew better than most that life can be rough and unfair. In her fierce black pride she was a living testament of resilience, grit, determination, and resolve not to be defeated by life's racist bullies. Due to her uncanny sense of timing that day, her intuition that this situation called for action on my part rather than sympathy on her part, I was forced to master an interpersonal problem from which I gained confidence in my own physical strength and in my ability to take care of myself.

Actually, this episode was one of several that occurred at a time in my childhood when, as a result of gymnastics training, I was transforming myself from an uncoordinated ninety-pound weakling into a person with some physical prowess. On the one hand, I regard this new physical mastery as an important milestone in my growth as a young male in this culture. On the other hand, the episode with Carl leaves me with a sense of incompletion and sadness. I hear no background strains of the theme song from the movie *Rocky* when I remember my triumph. Poor Carl was no doubt acting out of some personal internal suffering, doing unto life what life had, in some cruel way, done unto him. Even at age nine I sensed this, and my victory was dampened by this awareness. Later in life I would come to recognize that my solidarity in suffering with my enemy, Carl, as well as with my heroine, Charlie Mae, was a profoundly Christian attitude. I would also come to realize much later that in my capacity for sadness in this situation was the kernel of something much more valuable than physical strength, something deep within me that could become an alternative basis for security. As we shall see later in this chapter, there is a power in the capacity for sorrow and mourning that is superior to the power of mastery when it comes to achieving security.

At the time of my battle with Carl, however, there was no adequate interpretation of my inner experience. There was some laughing and celebration over my victory, but nothing to address the terrible pathos I experienced. I secretly wondered, Why is the world this way? Why do there have to be bullies in the first place, and why is beating them up the only way to treat them? It all seemed so sad. Nevertheless, the "tough guy" mentality of my upbringing in a culture of rugged individualism and fierce competitiveness regarded such sorrowfulness as misplaced. Despite its obvious origin in Christian imagery, the term "bleeding heart" had negative connotations in my otherwise "Christian" neighborhood.

In chapter 1 some of the social forces that make overcoming insecurity a difficult challenge were identified. One of these forces is the prevailing attitude that elevates autonomy and deprecates dependency. The mastery principle that operates in us internally is the psychological counterpart to this societal hyperindividualism. Total belief in mastery leads to the conviction that life can be conquered, that only the strong survive, and that security comes by overcoming weakness and by getting even with the powers that have hurt us. This unending process of striking back at life, this blind repetition of suffering, is what the apostle Paul referred to as the "law of sin and death" at work in us. Far from providing lasting security, this policy of mastery leaves us with a legacy of fear and the need for defense. What is the alternative? If security does not come from being stronger, from what does it come?

Memory, Mourning, and Transformation

Nearly every day in counseling practice I see someone struggling to master an insecurity who is simultaneously avoiding some deep, gut-wrenching sorrow. Mastery becomes the substitute for mourning. This is quite understandable. Mourning is no fun. It is hard work. We even use the phrase "grief work" to describe the process of mourning a person must go through following a significant loss. We don't want to mourn because we do not want to have to reexperience our hurt and the feelings of vulnerability and weakness that accompany hurt. We prefer getting even to feeling sad. As one of my counselees put it, "It's easier for me to be mad than sad." Our culture discourages mourning. Time and again following massive loss, people are urged by their loved ones to "snap out of it" when their grief lasts more than a few weeks. Even in instances of colossal loss, such as the death of a child or a spouse of forty years, our culture frowns on extended grief. At the same time, because of its breakdown, the extended family provides less of a support system than ever before.

We simply do not like sorrow. The meaning of Jesus' beatitude "Blessed are those who mourn" (Matt. 5:4) is lost on this culture. The gospel is infused with the American insistence on positive thinking and with the cultural wisdom that "winning isn't everything, it's the only thing." We hate to lose, and we don't like to recount our losses. We don't want to mourn. Who wants to cry? It's humiliating and painful and makes us feel helpless.

What happens, however, to a person who cannot cry? What becomes of the individual who loses the capacity to grieve? Or, to put the question differently, What is the role of mourning in achieving security? This is precisely the form in which the question has been challenging me in recent years. Although pastoral counseling involves helping people master their life problems, I have noticed an important paradox: it is most often by remembering and mourning, rather than by planning and executing, that the most profound and lasting solutions to life's thorniest problems come to us. Planning for future change is most effective when it is preceded by remembering and mourning.

The whole concept of mourning has become central to my life and work. Counseling itself is a remembering and mourning process. In speaking of mourning, I am referring not only to actual losses, such as the death of someone important to us; I am speaking also of the symbolic losses to self-esteem and to security that occur when we are hurt or deprived by someone important to us. I am thinking of those life events which left us empty inside, those experiences which rendered us afraid and, later, defensive.

Mourning assumes and requires memory. In order to mourn our past, we must first remember our past. Remembering can be a difficult and painful experience. Like mourning, remembering can involve hard mental and emotional work. People who come for counseling are often amazed at how difficult it can be to remember childhood. Their early years of life are often a blur. But as they begin the process of self-reflection that defines counseling, they find that gradually their memories are engaged and certain crucial events and people from the past emerge into consciousness. The difficulty is that, while some of the memories are pleasant, many are painful. They possess an emotional component of sadness, fear, or rage. Perhaps this is why we don't remember the past, or why we only remember the good things.

Tom's memory was tinged with nostalgia when he wrote his poem "Where Are You, Norman Rockwell?" He believed his distant past to be somehow care-free. In counseling, however, he became conscious of the real hurts in his childhood. All was not as rosy and happy as his nostalgic mood had implied. Remembering challenges us emotionally, as we recall the feelings of insecurity we experienced at those occasions of emotional abandonment or suffocation in childhood.

While remembering can be painful, it is the alternative to repeating the past. Those who cannot or will not remember are destined to repeat. Remembering first calls a halt to the repetition compulsion. Second, remembering helps us to conceive of our own life as a narrative, replete with themes and plots, character development, and climactic moments. In other words, it is through memory that we become aware of our own life story. What is your story? You cannot answer that question without remembering. Only your capacity for remembering enables you to have a story at all. In a real sense, my goal in this book is to engage your memory. It is to get you to think about your life story. Why? Because after remembering your story, and then thinking of it in terms of the theme of insecurity, you will introduce something new into the unfolding drama of your own life.

This goal is not easy to attain, because inducing you to remember your story means bidding you to mourn. While remembering, you will get in touch with things that make you sad, just as my story of my encounter with Carl the bully, while certainly not my most profound sorrow, is for me filled with pathos. There is something about the mourning process that is both cleansing and transformative.

An influential book in my work with mourning comes not

from the realm of psychology but from biblical scholarship. Walter Brueggemann, in *The Prophetic Imagination,* tells us that the prophetic tradition from Jeremiah's laments to Jesus' weeping over Jerusalem emphasizes the fact that grief is the beginning of prophetic criticism. Anguish, not anger, is the prophetic idiom.[3] Sorrow paves the way for newness and change. What was psychologically true of Jeremiah and Jesus is also true for you and me. In the emotion of sadness, we separate ourselves from the numbing repetition of mastery and become aware, at a feeling level, that something in our life is not right. It is when we begin to feel this sadness about our situation, and grow weary of the repetition and failed efforts at mastery, that we come to the threshold of change. Security cannot come until we recognize that our current methods of achieving it are simply not working. Mourning begins the dismantling of our obsolete arsenal of defense.

An oft-repeated fear of counselees is "If I start crying, I'll never be able to stop!" Most of us have this big cry inside, but seldom does our social world afford permission, much less an opportunity, for the ache in our heart to find relief. Seldom do we allow the tears to flow. Mourning makes us vulnerable, hence the need for a safe setting and a trusted someone with whom to share our sorrow.

Three kinds of losses must be mourned in order to pave the way for a new basis of security. First, we must mourn those actual interpersonal traumas that convinced us the interpersonal world is dangerous. Second, we must mourn the loss of what we never had, yet desperately needed. Both these griefs involve the use of our imagination and the development of an ability to truly empathize with ourselves. Third, having mourned both our hurts and our deprivations (the dual reasons for the erection of our defense system), we can begin to grieve for the loss of these defenses as we relinquish them. This final grief is simultaneously an experience of joy and relief.

Licking Our Wounds

Some grief actually takes the form of remembering and reliving traumas from the past. Mary courageously engaged in this kind of mourning as she recalled and relived the cold showers, the terror of seeing her home surrounded by a forest fire, and the excruciatingly painful time when her parents' marriage was threatened by the presence of her father's mistress. One technique to assist the grieving process is to ask the individual to reenter the painful memory by way of imagination, only this time as an advocate or a resource person for his or her child self. For example, Mary had a painful memory of an experience with her mother that seemed to typify the entire relationship. When her father's mistress was living at the ranch, Mary remembers trying to comfort her mother, who she knew was suffering greatly. Once when she reached out to hold her mother's hand, her mother pulled away and hissed, "Don't touch me!"

This rejection of her gesture of love was singularly devastating to Mary. Even twenty-five years later, the very memory of it was excruciating. I asked Mary to imagine herself reaching out to help the eleven-year-old Mary of the memory. What would she say to young Mary? What would she want to do for her? Mary imagined holding her eleven-year-old self, comforting and reassuring her with words that recognized the validity of her love for her mother and addressed young Mary's awful feelings of insecurity regarding her parents' marital strain. Mary tenderly whispered soothing words to her own child self like "It's OK. It's not your fault. You're going to be all right." In this exercise, Mary was engaged in a constructive mourning process in which she was both reexperiencing her pain and simultaneously soothing her own heartache.

Perhaps you can recall similar painful experiences of rejection, abandonment, misunderstanding, loneliness, or loss in either childhood or adolescence. Think of one of your worst moments. Now, what word or act of kindness would you offer your child self to help relieve the pain? Can you imagine taking that young you by the hand or even in your arms and saying a word of comfort, reassurance, or acceptance? This is not easy for most of us. Certainly, it helps to have someone else provide this kind of empathy for us. In fact, the next chapter will explain that, to find ultimate security, our inner child must be "found," so to speak, accepted, and held in love by a transcendent source. Nevertheless, there is an inherent value in being able to soothe oneself, and such self-soothing may actually be the beginning of self-transcendence and even of religious trust.

Opening the eye of our imagination to see our own child self in interpersonal danger may actually occasion both a profound empathy for our own hurting selves and a healing union with our Creator and Redeemer, with whom, in that moment, we share the seeing. Even when God "seems" absent in our early story, as was the case for Mary, a mysterious and holy presence may be discerned in retrospect. One of the miracles of the process of memory and mourning is that it can become the medium for what I call "retroactive providence."

What is retroactive providence? I am overcome with grief when I hear a person recount enduring some tragedy as a child without any help from another person. The nagging question, "Where was God?" haunts me, and I am sorely tempted to doubt the existence of a loving God. Then I am confronted with the miracle of memory and its transcendence of time. I am reminded of the power of mourning to lead "back to the future" and to the rewriting of history. A string of events in the life of an individual becomes, in the process of remembering and mourning, a meaningful life story. Of course, memory of the brute facts alone does not yield this result. A larger, contextual "story" is presumed, the consciousness of which shall be discussed in chapter 5

Once an individual begins healing through the self-compassion and retroactive providence that are operative in this kind of remembering and mourning, it becomes possible to forgive the past and, as a result, become liberated from the compulsion to repeat it. Empathy and forgiveness are then extended to include the very persons who wounded us. You will remember that Mary's guilt was so intense she truly believed it would be unfair if she found happiness while her mother did not. This conviction revealed Mary's psychological embeddedness and entrapment in her mother. However, once Mary began to mourn over her many wounds, including those inflicted by her mother, she was able to extend her mourning to include her mother's wounds as well.

Mary grieved deeply and openly as she moved "into the pathos" (the literal meaning of "empathy") of her mother's loss of her own mother when she was only eight years old. This paved the way for a dramatic shift from "solidarity in misery" with her mother toward forgiveness of this mother who, out of her own woundedness, had wounded Mary. This new attitude of forgiveness allowed Mary to achieve an appropriate psychological separation. She was still linked to her mother, but in a new way. Through her new posture of forgiveness, she shared a solidarity in sin, in suffering, and in grace with both her mother and the rest of humanity. To forgive another is to recognize a common bond, a common weakness, a common humanity. As Mary said in her final counseling session, "I realize we're all together in this thing called life."

When We Get Stones for Bread

A still more difficult mourning than that involving memories of actual hurts is that which has to do with deprivations. It is more difficult because we are on less certain footing. It is one thing to recall being abused or unfairly treated by a parent or caretaker and quite another to be plagued by a sense that, somehow, something was just missing, that a response we needed was simply not forthcoming.

How are we to mourn the loss of what we never had or, at least, never had enough of? Some people are torn between rage toward those upon whom they depended for love, on the one hand, and, on the other hand, an awkward guilt over the lack of any hard evidence of abuse. These good folk say to themselves, "How can I justify feeling bad about my past? My suffering is nothing compared to that of others who were really hurt."

I once had real difficulty with Jesus' analogy in the Sermon on the Mount between divine love and parental love. "What man of you, if his son asks him for bread, will give him a stone? . . . If you then, who are evil, know how to give good gifts to your children, how much more will your Father who is in heaven give good things to those who ask him!" (Matt. 7:9, 11). This question follows the "Ask and it will be given you" passage in the sermon. Having heard story after story of parental neglect, I thought this quote revealed real naïveté. Ninety percent of the people who come to me for counseling have pockets loaded with stones, their backs bent and bowed by the weight of them, when all they were asking for was the bread of love! It finally occurred to me that Jesus knew this about human nature. His question is at once straightforward and terribly ironic in its analogy. More than a handful of fathers in his audience that day must have squirmed, relieved that the question was rhetorical and hence no cause for hemming and hawing. No preacher would dare choose this text for a Father's Day sermon. "What man among you?" indeed! In Jesus' hands, a simple religious analogy could simultaneously pack a prophetic wallop!

Parental sins of commission, such as punishing children unfairly for crimes they did not commit, are easier to identify and rail against than the sins of omission and neglect. What is one to do about memories of needing a hug good night but never getting it? Of yearning to be understood and thought of as special by a parent or sibling but, instead, simply finding oneself being ignored or taken for granted? Or desperately wanting to see your father's eyes light up with pride but, instead, having a father who seldom made eye contact at all?

Many have suffered massive deprivation of love, attention, succor, and help. They may not have had stones hurled at them, but they were handed emotional stones at key moments when they needed emotional bread.

In many cases this occurred simply because the parent or caregiver was too self-absorbed to be emotionally present for the child. Some parents are like stellar black holes in that their self-centeredness is a center of gravity sucking everyone else into their narcissistic sphere of influence. While they never intentionally hurt their children, neither do they actively know and love them for who they are in their own right. For children who resist being defined as orbiting planets around the parental star, the interpersonal universe from then on can be a vast, cold emptiness. They know something important was missing during childhood but are hard pressed to name it. When they do name it, they feel vaguely guilty for having done so.

Mourning the loss of what we never had enough of also strains our empathic imagination. It is harder to remember specific events of deprivation than actual traumas. Still, most of us do possess a mental ideal of what parental love should be. It is a love that knows when to hold us (and how tightly and for how long) and when to let us be alone (to pull away or to prove we can take care of ourselves). It is a love that enjoys us for who we are in our own right, that counts us as special yet does not hold us to impossible expectations. It is a love that makes us feel both secure and free at the same time. This love believes in us when we lack confidence in ourselves and forgives us when we've done wrong. This love looks after us, watches over us, and smiles upon us. Parental love puts us first, seeks our best interest, yet also looks forward with hope and without regret to that day of mutuality when we can love as equals.

Did you get enough of this love? Your sense of personal security depended on your getting enough. There are many people who, although they didn't receive nearly enough of this mature, unconditional, parental love, nevertheless have managed to live splendid lives. These individuals amaze and humble me. Yet even in the midst of living enormously creative and generous lives, their history of deprivation haunts and depletes and threatens to overwhelm them. Their self-doubt stems from a root dread that the "not-enoughness" of their original world translates into their own "not-enoughness" as persons. They feel like imposters who at any moment will be caught and exposed.

These persons fear that if they begin to mourn the loss of what they possess only tenuously (at best a highly conditional and brittle form of parental love), they may lose themselves in the process. The stones of neglect stored in their pockets are, they believe, the only things anchoring them to earth. More than others, perhaps, they need to be held while they mourn. Where does one find the requisite moorings for such mourning? If one is fortunate, a good marriage can provide the context, or perhaps an unusually trust-filled friendship or counseling relationship or an authentic Christian community. Mystically, for some, it is found in a trusting faith in God.

Mourning the loss of what one never sufficiently had but, nonetheless, needed is a strange and trying grief. It is less likely to result in forgiveness of the past than other sorrows precisely because the mourner is not certain what or whom to forgive. For those with selfish and childish parents, mourning the past can be doubly difficult. Especially is this so when those same parents become, in their old age, the burden of care and responsibility of those very children whom they eclipsed with their egotism. Here we have stones upon stones. It's an onerous thing to be obliged to honor the father or mother in old age who failed to love you in your youth. Still, the commandment holds. What is required is not some sentimental, phony, or forced forgiveness of your selfish parent, but raw courage to do what is right. The mourning of life's deficits, if we've got the guts to lean into it, stretches us to new heights of being human. An exquisite joy comes in the quiet knowledge that you have loved more than you were loved. It is like participating in a secret miracle: knowing, for example, that your children are receiving more and better than you received. There is something replenishing about mourning that cannot be said of mastering. There is something liberating about it as well. You are a free woman or man when you can "do unto life as you would have life do unto you." Maybe that is what Jesus meant in that most puzzling yet most promising beatitude, "Blessed are those who mourn."

A Farewell to Arms

Mourning, not mastery, ushers in the changes that make security possible. One of the great paradoxes of our human experience is that it is when we let go, not when we hold tighter or work harder, that change occurs. The mastery principle, when applied to noncompetitive interpersonal relationships, simply promotes the status quo. Mourning, on the other hand, introduces something new. In fact, mourning involves me in a recognition that the status quo is *not* working, that something is awry, broken—lost and unrecoverable by my own efforts. It includes the realization that, despite all my best efforts at mastering my problems and anxieties, the foundational reasons for my insecurity in life remain unaddressed.

The posture of mourning announces a dramatic shift in attitude toward ourselves and the world. This shift is transformative. It empowers change. It redirects us toward new sources of security. In biblical language, mourning paves the way for *meta-*

noia, repentance. When we can begin to mourn the tragic consequences of our defensiveness and the weary repetition of our
sorry old patterns of getting even with the world, we become
open to change. It is paradoxical that, when we are stopped dead
in our tracks and brought weeping to our knees because we
simply cannot take another arthritic stride in life's marathon,
this is when we actually begin to glimpse the finish line and to
smell victory.

This fundamental change has far-reaching effects. It results in
other changes, including a reversal of perspective regarding
oneself in the world. No longer is the world the problem to be
fixed. No longer do I view the other person as the "project" to
be controlled or mastered or worked upon by me and changed
in ways that make me feel secure. Instead, I become the "project." My personal security hinges on what I do about myself,
not on how my interpersonal world adapts itself to my insecurities. I cannot overstate the radical importance of this shift in
perspective. The mastery principle, when applied to relationship, yields two related but equally uncreative and unsuccessful
alternatives. On the one hand, it may lead me to remain stuck
in a no-win competitive power struggle with my significant
others (spouse, parent, child, professional colleage, or business
associate). In this power struggle, I employ either my abandonment or absorption defenses, depending on which kind of anxiety is evoked. On the other hand, I may assume the role of
reformer of all the important people in my life. My defenses of
faultfinding and even crying uncle are useful to me in this role,
in that I am convinced they not only will protect me but may
get my partner to change, to mend her ways.

Couples in marital strife are notorious reformers. If they seek
counseling, it is often with the intent to get their partner to
change. This is human nature. Naturally, we are prone to be
more aware of what the other is doing wrong than of what
we ourselves do. It is hard to be objective about oneself. The
tendency is to regard our mate as the project. The marriage
counselor is confronted with the difficult task of getting the
individuals to examine themselves and to make themselves (not
their mate) the "project," the object of reform. For an individual
member of an unhappy marriage to achieve this shift in perspec-

tive, mourning both the marital wounds and the marital deprivations must first occur.

Mourning enables us to let go of the lifelong conviction that
from an emotional survival standpoint our interpersonal world
is utterly undependable. The tears of the big cry of mourning
dissolve that deeply buried, calcified internal connection, "Bad
me, bad world." The liberating import of this is that we are now
free to relinquish our defenses, or at least to imagine doing so.

With a "mastery" approach to my interpersonal world, I
blindly press ahead, repeating my same old defensive strategies
for achieving security or my offensive policy of reforming everybody in sight, but with mourning comes the possibility of dismantling my costly defense system. It is as if, in the context of
mourning, a new inner dialogue is established. I begin to observe
my habitual, compulsive defensiveness and call it into question.
It can be a tremendously freeing and joyful experience when, in
the midst of an emotional battle with someone important who
has heretofore represented abandonment or absorption, I am
able to shut down my automatic defense system, let go of my
need to defend, and introduce a new response. This is not tantamount to raising the white flag of surrender. It actually involves seeing both the conflict and my adversary differently
because I now see myself in a new light. Since I do not perceive
myself as threatened, I am no longer in a battle. Likewise, my
partner or friend or child ceases to be my adversary when I am
no longer so threatenable. Mourning begins the process of dissolving the threats from both within and without.

Mourning is the beginning of a farewell to arms and thus,
paradoxically, paves the way for joy and laughter. It is the
beginning, not the completion. For I must still confront the question of the fundamental dependability of life. Even the mourning
process seeks validation in a transcendent source. Without the
reassurance of a validation that is ultimate and therefore super-
sedes the approval or disapproval of my significant others, my
mourning and the relinquishing of my defenses could be regarded as foolishness. By dissolving the petrified governing concept, "Bad me, bad world," mourning opens me to the
possibility of experiencing the world as good. It does not, however, guarantee that my experience will be good. Suppose I open

myself to the possibility that love exists and then find myself in my new defenselessness shot down again by life. Then what will I say? If not already devastated, I would be tempted to kick myself mercilessly for my stupidity. Better that I had chosen machismo over mourning. Wiser that I had "done it unto life, before life did it unto me!" What I am suggesting is that mourning must be joined by an orienting faith, a deep trust that grows in the soil of new experience. This trust supplies the necessary confidence in mourning. In Paul's terms, it "persuades" us that life is dependable. It reassures with such allusions to transcendent validation as "It is God who justifies; who is to condemn?" (Rom. 8:33–34).

In chapter 5 I will address this question of transcendent validation, not an easy one to deal with in the age of the loss of transcendence. Still, we will reflect on achieving this kind of trust as we look at the steps that must accompany mourning if true security is to be found.

Questions for Reflection

1. In what ways do you see yourself "doing unto life what life has done unto you?" Are you getting even with life through any particular relationship, such as with your spouse or your child? Whom does that person resemble or represent from your past?

2. Try the empathy exercise mentioned in this chapter. Recall a painful episode from your childhood. What would you have said or done to comfort your child self? (Old photographs can aid in jogging your memory, and the exercise may be all the more meaningful if you involve a trusted person in it. What would he or she have done to comfort or rescue your wounded child self?)

3. Is it really possible or even desirable to forgive the past, with all its hurts and injustices? How does dealing with our past affect our sense of security now?

5

Trust and the Security of Attachment

Having begun to mourn your losses in life, those experiences that caused you to become insecure and defensive, now what? I can almost hear you asking, "Must I grieve indefinitely? Can't I get on with life and stop living in the past?" This chapter will address these valid questions by setting forth the remaining steps to achieving security.

Embodiment and the Dual Desires for Separation and Union

The opposing fears of abandonment and engulfment actually have positive counterparts in two opposing but equally human desires. On the one hand is the intense urge for separation. It is our nature as human beings to strive for separation, to long to establish ourselves as individuals. This desire is everywhere apparent. I certainly see it in my seventeen-year-old daughter's obvious longing to be her own person. Although economically tethered to home, she has been almost out of sight and on her own for the last year, since she got her own wheels and her own job. We miss her, but we understand the desire.

On the other hand, there is the equally strong desire for union. When we feel the burden of our separation, the loneliness of standing as an individual over against the world, we crave to be taken hold of and determined by another. We long to surrender ourselves, to merge into someone else, to be absorbed into something greater. Feeling the weight of life's decisions on our shoulders, we yearn to defer to someone wiser, to lean on someone else's shoulder, to depend on someone stronger, even to lose ourselves utterly in that someone.

American culture, with its admiration for individualism,

tends to support the first desire, for separation, but not the other. Separation is valued. Our society knows no limit to the ways you can express your desire for becoming an individual, being your own person, doing your own thing. The desire for merger, dependency, surrender, and other expressions of the longing for union, however, are granted a more narrow scope of expression.

Our society's distrust of interpersonal union poses a real problem for all of us when we begin to experience the loneliness of "being our own separate person." It causes many to go underground into the world of alcohol and drugs in the quest for impersonal sources of oceanic oneness. It makes others vulnerable to religious cults that promise mindless unity and the relinquishing of the will to the reverend leader. Some seek union with nature, a legitimate but impersonal experience of unity, which does not requite the deepest longings for personal bonding. As one reclusive, interpersonally wounded gentleman mused, "Nature doesn't reach out for you, but then again, it doesn't smite you down!" This man needed people but had suffered greatly in his life at the hands of those upon whom he depended. Nature provided sanctuary from the dangerous world of people. Nature, however, while generous with her beauty, could not return his love.

All this overemphasis on the individual in isolation that characterizes our culture aggravates our situation regarding our need for union. Nature has already accentuated our individuality by placing us in bodies, in envelopes of skin that separate us from each other. You are there alone in your body and I am here in mine as we try desperately to communicate what we think, what we see, and what we feel. If we try really hard, we may come close to understanding one another, but we never fully succeed. Not even husband and wife in closest sexual bond succeed in overcoming the brute fact of their embodiedness and the separation that always prevails.

Carson McCullers, in her novel *The Member of the Wedding,* tells the story of gangling, twelve-year-old Frankie's passage from childhood to adolescence during the summer of her brother's wedding. It is the story of lost innocence, of that insecure moment of separation from childhood, as this girl goes from being Frankie to F. Jasmine to Frances. The story captures her at that awkward transition phase in which she belongs neither to childhood nor to adulthood, at that moment when the child becomes excruciatingly conscious that she is separate from everyone, aware that her body makes her separate. In one scene with old Berenice, the black housekeeper who has become Frankie's surrogate mother, she ruminates. "Doesn't it strike you as strange," she asks, "that I am I, and you are you? I am F. Jasmine Addams. And you are Berenice Sadie Brown. And we can look at each other, and touch each other, and stay together year in and year out in the same room. Yet always I am I, and you are you. And I can't ever be anything else but me, and you can't ever be anything else but you. Have you ever thought of that? And does it seem to you strange?"

Wise old Berenice seems to catch Frankie's drift. "We all of us somehow caught. We born this way and that way and we don't know why . . ." she replies. "I born Berenice. You born Frankie. . . . And maybe we wants to widen and bust free. But no matter what we do we still caught. Me is me and you is you. . . . We each one of us somehow caught all by ourself. Is that what you was trying to say?"

By now, Frankie is on Berenice's lap. "Yet at the same time you almost might use the word loose instead of caught. Although they are two opposite words. I mean you walk around and you see all the people. And to me they look loose. . . . I mean you don't see what joins them up together."

In this poignant passage from McCullers's novel we see the dilemma present in our being bodies. There we see old Berenice, aware of her black skin, her embodied separateness, as a being— trapped, caught, absorbed, imprisoned. There is twelve-year-old Frankie, conscious of her embodiedness as a being—loose, estranged, abandoned, alienated from the world of other people. There we are, you and I, caught and loose, and in both we feel the weight or airiness of our separation, our isolation, our individuality. There we are, forever destined, it seems, to experience the negative side of our desire, absorption instead of union, abandonment instead of separation.

If our security in life depends in part on the quality of our relationships with others, how are we ever to find security if (1) our very embodiedness isolates us, (2) our culture reinforces our individualism, and (3) our individual experience of a dangerous world has led us to build a wall of defense? First, we mourn this state of affairs. We plunge ourselves into the pathos of our walled isolation. We weep at the sight of all the lonely people, crouching in their little individual prisons, peering longingly out two peepholes called eyes, wanting desperately to know and to be known, to touch and be touched, yet despairingly unable to visit one another's locked cells. Then, when the tears of mourning having cleansed our sight, we open our eyes and our hearts to a new vision of humanity, one quite different from this culture's view. This new vision involves (1) repentance regarding our hatred of our weakness, (2) a new attitude of acceptance of our dependency, and (3) the recovery of our lost inner child, our trusting true self.

Dependency and Attachment

Whether or not we ever experience union with another, the fact remains that we all experience "attachment" to others. Most of us have many attachments of varying intensity. We need attachment to survive. In fact, our attachments actually determine our humanity and our identity. Attachments—or relationships—are essential for human life. These attachments we need in order to thrive, however, are also the reasons for our insecurity. This is a great dilemma in our human existence: that we experience ourselves being destroyed by the very thing we need in order to live—attachment. It's like realizing that life itself is carcinogenic!

Many seek to escape the dilemma by denying the fact of our dependency on attachments. As indicated in chapter 1, our culture denies dependency, having developed a "dependency phobia." We live and move and have our being in the midst of this cultural myth of self-sufficiency and rugged individualism. We actually believe there is such a person as the self-made man. Sooner or later, however, we realize that living in this myth has its drawbacks. We realize that our societal admiration of independence only aggravates the dilemma, leaving us painfully isolated and forsaken in our individualism.

It Takes Guts to Be Helpless and Needy

Achieving security inevitably involves a change of heart regarding our human weakness. We must reject the popular wisdom that suggests we can overcome our insecurities simply by becoming stronger within ourselves and by ourselves.

People who come for their first counseling session are frequently embarrassed and uneasy that they have done so. They may diminish the importance of their problems compared to the difficulties other people face. More often, they simply feel ashamed of themselves for not being able to solve their problems by themselves. I try to reassure these individuals of the courage it took actually to seek help. The irony, of course, is that getting help takes guts, precisely because it involves a departure from our belief in self-sufficiency.

William Lynch, writing that hope and help are intricately related, says that the whole notion that we must depend only on ourselves is nothing short of a cultural lie.[1] He expresses a conviction I share when he says, "I believe that our need for help is deeply inscribed in every part of us and is identical with our human nature. The need and the fact is so strong, powerful and characteristic that it can be frightening (especially if its first childhood manifestations have been traumatic or sharply frustrating)."[2] Indeed, our need for help can be frightening, which is precisely why it requires courage to seek it.

Culturally, we must repent of the lie of self-sufficiency, a lie that relegates too many needy people to lives of quiet desperation. As individuals, we must cease being ashamed of our weakness and of our need for help. No group in this culture is more free and undaunted by the cultural stigma of weakness than Alcoholics Anonymous. Contrary to popular misinterpretation, A.A. is not a self-help organization; recognizing their own helplessness, members of A.A. help one another. A person's true entry into A.A.'s recovery process begins with the gutsy admission, "I am an alcoholic. I am powerless over alcohol." Only with this confession can the chains of addictive denial be loosened.

Something essentially the same as this alcoholic confession is required if we are to overcome our insecurity. "I am an insecure person. For all my bravado, deep down I am weak, frightened, and needy. I am powerless over my insecurity. I need help." Some of us will choke on our pride when we hear ourselves actually saying these words, but with practice it gets easier. We even begin to sense that this confession is the starting point for getting out of our dilemma. It is reassuring to realize that recognizing and accepting our weakness is not tantamount to losing our autonomy and strength. On the contrary, repentance toward our weak and needy selves constitutes a giant step toward secure selfhood, freedom, and personal empowerment.

Accepting the Fact of Our Dependence

The question is not whether or not we are dependent but how we express our basic dependency. We are all basically dependent. Not only do we begin and end life this way, we remain dependent all our lives, even at our peak of personal creativity and influence. No matter how strong we appear, underneath we are all fragile creatures. Given enough stress, any of us could break. We are all vulnerable to being exposed in our personal weakness. Regardless of how independent we seem, our dependency is always a fundamental fact of our existence. While there are some incredibly resourceful individuals in this world, there are no self-made men or women. Everyone depends ultimately on someone or something else.

The primary human motivation is the drive to relate, to establish a connection with another. It is the psychological equivalent of the biological drive to eat or to breathe. People who need people are not only lucky, they are human. That we become a human self at all is by virtue of our attachments. From the very beginning, we depend on others not only for our physical survival but for our very self-definition and self-determination. I know who I am becoming, in part, because of the way my father and mother behold me as I grow. Their smiling or disapproving eyes are the mirror before which I practice my dance steps and evolve my unique style. Furthermore, their steps and style become a part of my own. This is not only because I have inherited their genes, but also because I incorporate their very personalities into my own. They provide the personal stuff of which I am being composed, they and my siblings and my teachers and my friends and my heroes and my enemies through the years. I am dependent on them all.

No one writes a life story alone. As the Kentucky poet Wendell Berry wrote in his essay, "Men and Women in Search of Common Ground":

> Each of us has had many authors, and each of us is engaged, for better or worse, in that same authorship. We could say that the human race is a great coauthorship in which we are collaborating with God and nature in the making of ourselves and one another. . . . This is only a way of saying that by ourselves we have no meaning and no dignity; by ourselves, we are outside the human definition, outside our identity.[3]

There exists no individual to be known apart from his or her attachment to others and no people to be known apart from their relationship to their Author.

We are dependent on one another for the very authorship of our lives. In one respect, this makes our significant others very powerful. As our coauthors, it would appear they hold our fate and our esteem in their hands. To an extent, this is true, but it is not an awful truth if I remember that they too are dependent on me. I am also *their* author. This fact of our mutual dependency does not have to evoke fear and defensiveness, despite the fact that our earliest experiences of being helpless and dependent were crushingly disappointing.

My being dependent on others for my own sense of self is not threatening if I am aware of the fact that all these dependencies are relative, not absolute. I am greatly helped in this if I have a faith in an absolute source of my dependence, a faith in God, my attachment to whom guarantees my worth, strengthens my selfhood, and validates my being here. Regarding my dependent attachments as "relative" helps me to achieve the necessary perspective for being secure rather than endangered in my attachments.

For instance, I would imagine you have been saying to yourself, "OK, suppose I begin to mourn my losses, drop my defenses, and open myself to new possibilities in my relationships. What happens if my significant other does not? Suppose he or she remains defended or needs to repeat the past in order to get back at life through me? In other words, how can I risk changing if my spouse, my parent, my child, or my co-worker does not?"

Sally, for example, wanted very much to become more secure in herself in her new marriage to Bud. She wanted to be less defensive, but she felt Bud was extremely judgmental. She resented that he was especially critical of her parenting strategies with her children by a former marriage. Because she lacked confidence in her mothering skills, one little hint of his disapproval could ruin her entire day. Fearing abandonment, she would deploy a "leave before you're left" defense, and soon tension between her and Bud escalated into outright warfare. Sally worked hard in counseling to affirm the relativity of her dependence upon Bud. She realized she needed his approval, but that his opinion of her mothering techniques was not going to make or break her as a mother. She also recognized that Bud was actually less critical than she was of herself in this regard and that his opinion was actually triggering her own self-criticism. As she began to affirm her own parenting abilities (making her own insecurity, not Bud's judgmentalism, the project), she was able (1) to reaffirm that Bud's suggestions were often quite constructive and (2) to maintain her inner balance even when Bud seemed out to reform her.

Sally enjoyed her newfound security. She also derived a quiet satisfaction from knowing—as we all can know—that her partner, upon whom she depended for love and self-validation, was not the enemy. Even a partner's defensiveness can occasion our growing more secure in ourselves. This strengthening could not occur were we not dependently attached to begin with. In marriage and in any other important relationship, we are dependent on both the bad and the good which the other brings to his or her co-authorship of our lives.

Marriage in our culture has become what Ernest Becker calls "the cosmology of two."[4] That is to say, given the loss of an active belief in God as Creator, couples have come to expect the marriage relationship to deliver what, in former times, would only have been asked of God. The cultural belief regarding marriage seems to be that my partner holds the key to my salvation, my self-worth, and my ultimate validation as a person. This is simply too much to ask of the marriage relationship. It is misplacing ultimate dependency needs on a finite human being, our mate.

Sally began to feel freedom to fail in Bud's eyes when she began to anchor herself once again in her long-standing faith in God's unconditional love for her. As her self-confidence was restored, she became less defensive in response to Bud's criticisms, and he became less critical! It dawned on her that he too depended on another for approval—her. She realized one of the great mysteries of attachment, that security begets security.

Recovering Your True Self

While memory and mourning lead to an acceptance of the enoughness of life and to a letting go of defenses, it is also important that we recover our own repressed or forgotten true self, our own lost inner child. This is the part of us that withdrew from interaction with the world because of our experience of the danger of attachments. The true self hated its dependence because it experienced the interpersonal world as undependable. This is the part of us that went into hiding. It has been incubating all this time, awaiting a better, safer world. Our hidden inner child is the source of our original energy and purpose. Its heart is the stronghold of our creativity, the safe deposit box of our true talent. To the extent that our true self is hidden away, cut off from the rest of our personality, to that same extent we are deprived of power and energy to live life.

Our inner child, or true self, is also our insecure, needy self, which has sought refuge from its need and from a cold depriving world where stones are passed off as bread. This fact partially explains why we have such difficulty recovering our true self. It may appear to us ugly in its raw neediness and grotesque in its life of neglect, like some derelict orphan or stranger, rather than the long-lost talent that it is.

How do we recover this lost child of ours? We may engage in the kind of remembering that was described in chapter 4, a compassionate remembering. Also, we can examine now what it is we truly desire, what we have needed from life all along.

Recovering our true self may require determination and even a certain self-centered resolve. It may even involve finding someone to hear us out, someone who will listen to our story and help us listen for the cries of our lost inner child. Mary was always putting other people's needs first. In part, this was her way of earning love and of establishing some sense of goodness. She once had a dream, however, in which her lost inner child said to her from her reflection in a mirror, "You'll have to tend to my needs before you serve others!" The truth of the dream is in its realization that to give ourselves to others we must first have a self. How can we give to others if our own true self has never been born into the world but, rather, has remained hidden and neglected, waiting for a more inviting and receptive atmosphere in which to thrive?

There is truth in the paradoxical idea that progress often occurs through regression. Jesus knew this when he told us that to enter the kingdom of God we must become as little children (Luke 18:15–17). Recovering the true self may well actually entail allowing our imprisoned, hidden, withdrawn inner child to come out and sing and dance and play. Or an even deeper regression may be needed, a labor that may have been aborted by too much suffering early on in life requiring that we "must be born anew" (John 3:7).

Our inner child, in addition to being both our true (and needy) self, is also our trusting self. It is our original, pristine, defenseless response, our as-yet-unharmed inner child who, having no reason to doubt, trusts without reservation, without hesitation, without flinching. Perhaps, owing to a lifetime of scars, we can never trust so purely, so completely again as when we were a sleeping child, awash in our mother's lullaby. Maybe the habitual defensiveness now acts as a reflex. Still, it is possible to increase our trust and lower our defenses so that we are not ruled by our fatalistic impulse.

When intimidated, I may reflexively reach for my gun, but if it is not loaded, or, better still, if it was long ago beaten into a plowshare, I simply must resort to a new way of responding to threat. This "new way" includes recovering a relationship to that original capacity for trust. What I have perceived as threats in my life have often proven to be otherwise. Trigger-fingered scaredy-cat that I've been most of my life, I have too often found myself shooting at my own elongated shadow, not at any real threat. By reconnecting with my trusting self, I am less prone to look for trouble where it doesn't exist. My characteristic supervigilance has given way to a more relaxed approach to life, even to those inevitable real threats and conflicts that come along. I've been able to holster my six-gun, having dropped from first to twenty-sixth fastest draw in the West, and I look forward to retiring it altogether. Maybe I'll pawn it for a good book about overcoming insecurity!

By opening myself to trusting again, I simultaneously open myself to the "good." Likewise, by opening myself to experiencing the good, which in my defensiveness I have kept at arm's length along with the "bad," I build up my capacity for trust. What is the good and how do I allow myself to encounter it?

Incorporating the Good

You will recall that our first, most primitive defense against the bad in life is to internalize it, take it into ourselves and repress it into our unconscious, along with that piece of ourselves which is historically related to it. There is no one single "childhood trauma" but, rather, a whole history of experiencing our interpersonal world as bad—bad, that is, from an emotional survival standpoint. This original defense, however, left us guarded and frightened and fostered an arms race between us and our interpersonal world.

How do we counteract the effects of this original defense? A negative internalization must be counteracted by a positive one. If the bad that was outside is now inside, wreaking its havoc, it stands to reason that the remedy involves an internalization of the good. In this case, however, I prefer the term "incorporation." Since I am embodied, the good is internalized not merely intellectually but taken into my whole self, into every fiber of my being. I must incorporate it. It becomes heart knowledge as well as head knowledge. If I am to become secure, I have to let the good all the way in. To incorporate it is to take it to the bank emotionally, to deposit it irrevocably in my being.

Recovering our lost and needy true self is not something we can easily achieve alone. It helps to have a "good enough other": friend, spouse, mentor, father or mother figure. I need someone who cares about me, wants to know the real me, and therefore invites out my true self. You may have such a person or persons in your life already. They may be there, but your own defensiveness prevents you from seeing their basic goodness and from incorporating it.

Perhaps that "good enough" other person hurt or disappointed you once so, demanding perfection, you shut the door permanently. Open the door again. Let that person's goodness enter you, minister to your neediness, call forth your true self. If there is no such person currently in your life, find one. In your search, do not look for perfection but rather for goodness, for someone who is basically trustworthy, understanding, realistic, honest, and secure.

We need to incorporate the good out there in order to dissolve the bad we took inside early on, to diminish its influence. Many of us are reluctant to open ourselves to the good for fear the bad will sneak in with it. We indiscriminately defend against good and bad. For instance, someone whose opinion matters to you pays you a compliment, you say "thank you" politely, but internally you brush aside the affirming words. The compliment may actually make you very uncomfortable.

Dropping defenses allows you to accept the compliment, to receive the good from your relationships. The tricky part is that, to receive the good, you must be willing to drop your defenses, despite the fact that bad comes with the good. Yes, that same "good enough" other can and will hurt you from time to time, sometimes intentionally but more often because of personal insecurity. This person is boxing with shadows and your emotional jaw got in the way! To incorporate the good that is present in any relationship—a marriage, a parent-child attachment, even a professional colleagueship—we must be willing to risk the bad in order to receive the good. This is human life. This is accepting that life, love, and all attachments are imperfect.

It Helps to Have Received Perfect Love

For most of us, coming to a position of inner security that stoically accepts life's many imperfections is simply not an option, because the imperfections have hurt us too badly. They have mortally wounded us. These interpersonal wounds have left us too skeptical to open ourselves again, recklessly or naïvely. Nothing short of perfection will do.

This is why our security problems are ultimately religious in nature. They beg for a religious solution! Without recognition of an absolute source of our dependence, our relative dependencies on the significant people in our lives become absolute and therefore dangerous. The badness in them also takes on an absoluteness. Every verbal exchange in which I am criticized by my important other becomes, for me, "judgment day." Every experience of disapproval or rejection becomes a final condemnation. If I am not conscious of an absolute source, I am apt to regard the key people who populate my emotional world in ultimate terms as either God or the devil.

The great nineteenth-century theologian Schleiermacher told us that the very essence of religion was the "feeling of absolute dependence." His word for God, or that upon which we and the universe depend absolutely, was the "Whence" of our dependence.[5] All of us are capable of this "feeling of absolute dependence," but we tend to suppress it in our everyday lives; in this secular and allegedly sophisticated age of science, materialism, and hyperindividualism, we tend to deny it altogether. When suppressed or denied, the feeling gets misplaced and shows up in our relative dependencies. When this occurs, it predictably makes us miserable, destined for disappointment, and eternally enslaved by our dependencies.

The American culture's myth of self-sufficiency would actually be the more logical and prudential basis for living were there no "Whence" worthy of our worship. The well-defended life, moreover, would be the only good life. Genuine God-consciousness, unsuppressed and undenied, on the other hand, makes possible the dropping of defenses and the incorporation of the good. Awareness of God can accomplish this to the extent that this "Whence" of our dependence is simultaneously felt to

be dependable. In other words, we can incorporate the love of
the coauthors of our lives, despite the ambiguity of their love,
if somewhere, someway, somehow, we are the recipients of a
higher love—a perfect, unadulterated, unambiguous, un-
reserved, utterly uninhibited love, the love which God alone can
provide.

With the consciousness of an absolute source of love comes
liberation from the fear that plagues our attachments, provided
that this absolute love is incorporated. This divine love is the
way out of the dilemma of being destroyed by the very thing we
need, attachment. It supplies a perspective, a transcendent reference point from which to gauge and adjust the degree of our
dependency on others. This incorporated divine love enables us
to live within and even to be coauthored by our relative dependencies without being utterly determined by them. As the ultimate determinant of our identity and self-worth, it puts an end
to that danger of attachment discussed in chapter 2. As a New
Testament writer puts it, "There is no fear in love, but perfect
love casts out fear" (1 John 4:18).

How do we incorporate this love? For that matter, how do we
incorporate the love of our mentor, our friend, our mate?
Mainly it involves an attitude of active receptivity, an openness
to the possibility of the good. It calls for a narrative interpretation of life wherein all events—good and bad, comic and
tragic—are regarded as relevant to my story and therefore worthy of being appropriated, written into the text.

During the course of writing this book, for instance, I've
taken up gum chewing as part of my effort to give up smoking
cigarettes. Recently, I made the happy discovery that a certain
old-fashioned chewing gum is back on the market. This gum has
a special significance for me in that it was my grandfather's
brand. J.K., as we knew him, delighted in giving out sticks of
this gum to all us grandkids whenever we were at his house, ever
extolling its laxative powers, much to our amusement and to our
parents' chagrin! I've been chewing it as though I owned stock
in the company, and in the process I have been flooded with the
fondest memories of this man who was one of the chief coauthors of my early story. There is a kind of corporeal quality to
these memories, enhanced in a way by the unique flavor of this

antique gum. I can also hear his voice, especially his guileless laughter, and replay his distinctive gestures in my mind's eye.

The memories of my grandfather, who quit smoking at forty, have been more soothing than gum-chewing alone would have been. It is as if this bodily memory of that grandfather whom I happily incorporated as a boy has provided a recollection of embodied goodness that is helping me now to conquer my worst bodily addiction. I am allowing a previous chapter in my life to have a bearing on my present one by seeing a connection between my story and that of one of my coauthors in life. If my hero J.K. could quit smoking, so can I!

One of the regular rituals of the church provides us with an experiential base of perfect love, the Lord's Supper. It is the occasion for remembering the Person and the sacrificial event of our salvation and healing. Again, the phenomenon of human memory plays a key role. We know about Christ and the Gospel story because these are carried by the memory of the New Testament writers and by the church throughout history. Somebody remembered the story. Happily, the memory of the good has been remembered for us throughout the centuries. There is something quietly reassuring about this memorial connection. At every communion service we reenact what has been remembered for us and which we are now remembering. It involves an incorporation of the good. "Take, eat, for this is my body which is given for you. Feed on me in your hearts with faith."

I can think of only two differences, really, between the memorial processes set into motion for me by a stick of my grandfather's brand of chewing gum and a communion wafer. The one is soothing, the other saving. That is to say, remembering J.K.'s gift of himself, symbolized in his generosity with gum, is a source of solace as I attempt to cope with the nagging symptoms of my nicotine withdrawal. Remembering Christ's sacrifice is the reassurance that love prevails, that it is absolute, that the "Whence" of my absolute dependence, God, is also absolutely dependable because, says Christ's cross, God is love.

The second difference is that my memory of my grandfather is immediate, whereas my memory of Christ's sacrifice is mediated. I was actually present when that rare gum was being handed out. Not that my memory is completely trustworthy.

Certainly it is not perfectly objective, but I experience it as reliable and true. As regards the other memorial process, I am depending on the reliability of the memory of others. There is no escaping that a greater trust is required.

What if I am being deceived? What if this Christian story is, after all, a hoax or the result of a pleasant but infantile wish? On the other hand, what if all that is being remembered at every Lord's Supper is true? Then love prevails. By trustingly incorporating Christ, my story, along with its numerous intersections with my grandfather's story, is intersecting with a larger story, one that makes all of us, grandfathers and grandsons, grandmothers and granddaughters, members of the cast of the great drama of redemption.

When a person is open and trusting enough, this mediated experience of shared memory has itself a way of becoming immediate. Having dipped my toe in the great river of Christian memory, I am soon aware of the mysterious power of this memory to cut across calendar time, to make contemporaries of all its participants. The touching final communion scene in the movie *Places in the Heart* captured this mystery in a heartrending way when the camera panned the church pew to show both the living and the dead sharing the bread.

The bread we incorporate in Christian communion is good in that it is a symbol of the love of God for us. It speaks to our guilt in the form of forgiveness. It addresses our sense of abject, unconditional badness with unconditional acceptance. This love saves us even at the level of our ego weakness, addressing that part of us which is barely there, barely a self at all. It speaks to our weakness in three ways: first, through the notion of God's creation of our true self which awaits birth; second, through God's role as catalyst for our rebirth; third, as Christ becomes our chief coauthor in developing our character (Phil. 2:12–13). This bread is good. It is no stone.

Incorporation of this good bread gives birth to and then forms our person so that our true self flourishes. You will recall Mary's dream in which she was pregnant and I was her artistic husband (see chapter 2). She later came to see the figure of the artist as Christ who had created and who would deliver her true self into the world. She had another dream that reveals how she incorporated the good:

> I was in a large classroom with many women. We were being trained to become "mass women." The emphasis was all on external appearance. I felt out of place. Suddenly, I was in a group of radicals. I still felt out of place. The scene shifted back to the classroom. I felt I had to leave. I ran down an old staircase and was thinking to myself, I may have to be abandoned by everyone. On the staircase was a cookie. I knew it had been left there for me, so I picked it up and ate it.

In some respects the dream revealed, in digest form, Mary's lifelong struggle to feel secure in her feminine identity. The dream suggests that to find her true identity she will have to give up the false security of various mass definitions of womanhood in which she had submerged her true self. Doing this felt risky, like being abandoned. However, the dream offers a reassurance to her hungry, needy inner child in the cookie, a new symbol for Mary of the nurturing, person-forming presence of God.

What father, if his son asks him for bread or a cookie or a stick of chewing gum, will give him a stone? Not the father of our absolute dependence. The continuity with the past, the sense of belonging to the family of humanity, and the affirmation of our individual uniqueness are all aspects of "the good" of the Christian reality which, if incorporated, provides the basis for a secure life. For example, Mary once quite spontaneously revealed how this comes about. Contrasting her budding sense of security with the total rejection she felt as a child, she said, "I'm beginning to feel God in my gut. It's as if I have an assurance that my inner child is wanted. I guess this is what I've wanted most of all, to know that God wants me."

Seeing the "We of Me"

Experiencing a "defenseless" security in life involves a new attitude, a new perspective. It involves understanding my humanity in a radically different way from that of my culture's view. Earlier in the chapter, I suggested that it "seemed" that nature itself had conspired with our individualistic culture to render us utterly isolated in our embodied individuality. Further discussion of our natural dependency, our ubiquitous attachments and their coauthoring role in our lives, calls this hyperindividualism into question. To overcome our insecurity, you and I must call into question this view of ourselves as fundamentally separate entities. We need to come to see our connection with each other, to realize our interdependence.

A flashback to Carson McCullers's story of Frankie may help drive home this point. Frankie, you recall, felt estranged from everybody during that awkward time of puberty. She couldn't see what bound people together. They just seemed loose, unrelated and unattached. In the story, however, Frankie discovered a connection that summer of her brother's wedding. As she thought of her brother and his bride, it came over her so convincingly that she almost blurted out loud, *They are the we of me.* "Yesterday, and all the twelve years of her life," writes McCullers, "she had only been Frankie. She was an *I* person who had to walk around and do things by herself." Now all this had suddenly changed as Frankie realized what you and I must also realize, that we cannot be a self, we cannot even conceive of ourselves apart from those to whom we are connected, apart from those who are the *we* of our *me.* We bring to life, in our true self, an original, inimitable body of talent and personality. It is the raw material, which is shaped and molded and perfected in the relationships that constitute us.

The reassurance of this view of persons is the tremendous sense of belonging it offers. Nature, conceived as creation, does not conspire to isolate us but binds us to one another! The envelope of skin that separates us is not the final boundary; there is an intermingling of spirits, which in memory and mercy, compassion and cooperation, transcends body, time, and space. When we capture this vision of ourselves, defenses such as "standing outside of time" become obsolete because we realize that (1) there is no solitary me apart from my interconnectedness with others and (2) my finite here-and-now relationships are far more expansive than they seem, connecting me with all humanity.

When Mary came for counseling she told me, "Life is hell if

you're connected to someone and hell if you're not connected." Mary, who at one time echoed her counterdependent culture with her words, "I can leave any relationship and never feel anything," later came to a positive and liberating realization of her interconnectedness with God and others. She became involved in a church, was baptized, and later married. Toward the end of our time together she spoke of her realization of the "we" of her "me" in this way:

> I feel solid now, for the first time. I'm tapping into some creative part. I have energy to do things. It's like I'm beginning to feel God's grace. I keep thinking of that image, you know, when Christ said, "I am the vine, ye are the branches." I feel connected.

Mary's transformation was remarkable, a testimony to her courage and perseverance during the four years we worked together. She went from being a frightened, weak, disheartened, distrusting, and weary traveler to the confident, solid, energized, secure woman revealed in the above confession.

For you and me to conquer our insecurity, we must incorporate the good and appreciate our connection to the others in our lives. What I am saying, obviously, is that to overcome our insecurity we need a faith. In place of defensiveness and a policy of striking back at life we must put a trusting faith in a loving God. We develop this faith not in some ivory tower but in the thick of life, in the midst of our attachments, by dropping our defenses and opening ourselves to the possibility that our deepest needs for both separation and union can be addressed.

Persuasion and Trust

What would cause us to choose faith rather than defense as a basis for security? I began this book by recalling my loss of innocence regarding my own insecurity in an insecure world. I wish to address this faith question by recalling another chapter in my story of insecurity, a time ten years ago when I was in the midst of a divorce, a time for me of frightening disintegration and total insecurity.

In the first place, I could never in my wildest imagination

consider that I would ever be divorced. It was simply unthink-
able. Its becoming thinkable was, in itself, a shattering experience, a complete break with my self-concept. It also entailed a
devastating break with my familial and religious foundations.
Most cataclysmic of all, the exile and disillusionment that constituted the aftermath of divorce was for me the end of all trust
in God and in my connectedness to other human beings. Divorce, it seemed, was pervasive in its influence. Divorce was, for
me, not merely the ending of a marriage. It was divorce from
everybody and everything. Especially was I divorced from myself. I lost custody of my soul.

I was also divorced from my faith. There was no longer
anything palpable about the Christian memory. It was someone
else's memory and, for me, hand-me-down religion. Jesus
seemed detached and sometimes irrelevant, like a first-century
goody-two-shoes who in no way could identify with my pain.
After all, he was never even married, and in scripture he seems
to come down hardest on men in divorce.

Although science and secularism conspired to erode my
Christian faith, the greatest contributor to my doubt was precisely the spirit of radical individualism and counterdependence
that so dominates our culture and has worked in and upon my
own human strivings for security and self-definition. During this
dark and dreadful time in my life I was experiencing more
keenly than ever the separating, abandoning, rending effects of
this individualism. I was living alone in a small apartment,
grieving, struggling to adapt to my new situation in life. I would
awaken in the middle of the night and feel totally disoriented.
I would find myself sitting bolt upright in a cold sweat, my chest
heaving for breath and my pulse pounding in my head, in a state
of complete panic because I didn't know where I was or even
who I was. I was alone. While to some degree my exile was
self-imposed, to a great extent it was imposed by a social world
that simply did not know what to do with me. If you have been
through divorce, you know how isolating it can be. You feel
judged. Perhaps because of the threat your situation poses to
others whose marriages are shaky, you become a pariah.

One night I awoke in my usual panic, tripped around my dark
apartment looking for a light, feeling as though I was truly

losing my mind. This was more than a mental storm. Then, out of the corner of my eye, I saw Jesus sitting casually on my windowsill, arms crossed, head cocked. He was grinning from ear to ear, almost impishly, and seemed to wink just before he bounded from my window, disappearing into the night. Face pressed hard against the pane, I searched the darkness for my mysterious intruder. I knew I must be losing my mind!

What was happening to me? I sat on the edge of my bed and held myself, trying to take deep breaths to regain my composure. Then a thought occurred to me that changed everything. It was an imaginative idea. I wondered who else in this world of five billion people had awakened just now as I had, in a cold, sweaty panic, not knowing who they were, and, like myself, all alone. Suddenly a wave of peace came over me persuasively as I felt my connection and my solidarity with—even my belonging to—all those other lonely people out there. This feeling was restorative. Only a moment before, I had felt isolated and cut off from people, forsaken. In Frankie's word I was "loose," not joined to anyone. I was an individual unit of human consciousness, but as such I was fading out, losing myself, feeling that ego weakness which inevitably results when we attempt to define ourselves solely by our individuality. Now, with this wonderful intuition of my connection with others at the very point of our suffering from our common forlornness, came an almost instantaneous surge of strength and a renewal of faith. The "hallucination" of a few moments before became, in retrospect, a strange and wonderful visitation I shall never forget. That impish Christ had awakened me to my kinship with the night. I can only tell you that from that point forward Christ no longer seemed unfriendly or puritanical and certainly not irrelevant. Christ remains ever elusive, like on that night, but also ever present in my memory as a power, as an empowering consciousness of my connection to him and to his people.

How is this piece of my story an answer to the question of why faith rather than defense? It is an account of someone who, perhaps like yourself, wants both freedom and love, who wants to be able to stand on his own two feet yet be upheld in life. I am gambling on the fact that you are not so different from me. Perhaps you have tripped into God but have dismissed or even forgotten what you saw. We cannot prove God to one another, much less a loving God. The world is a horrifying place sometimes. If God is, and if God loves, why doesn't God do something to stop all the madness?

In telling you this piece of my story I'm banking on the possibility that if you can identify with my isolation you may also identify with that feeling of connection with your fellow humanity, with Christ, with that Higher Power upon whom you depend, as do I, for your next breath. I'm wagering that if I can feel my absolute dependence, so can you. There is no magic here. There is no infallible or scientific proof. There is what the apostle Paul called "persuasion." Paul, you remember, identified those powers which strike at our connections with one another, with our very selves, with God, with meaning, and with all our securities and then said simply, "I am sure that . . . [nothing] will be able to separate us from the love of God" (Rom. 8:38–39). Not even the sharp edge of death itself can sever us from our security.

What led Paul to so bold a profession of robust confidence, of absolute trust? What was his story?

Faith involves persuasion, not a guarantee. We still doubt. We still encounter great risks. Sometimes we get confused about God. Just as I had confused Jesus with some first-century Dudley Do-Right, we sometimes get God mixed up in our minds with someone else in our experience. We confuse God with the father who gives the stone. It appears that the world, if it is being run by a God, is being run by a capricious depriving deity, not a trustworthy God of love. Unless, of course, we are persuaded, as Paul was, that the sufferings of this life have no power to sever us from the love of God precisely because Christ's suffering gathers all other human suffering into its cross, Christ's forsakenness abolishes ours, and Christ's resurrection upholds those who are weak. It is a matter of persuasion. It is being persuaded by the good we see of the Good we cannot see—except sporadically, in mystic visitation or, more often, in corporate memory. It is daring to trust that life and relationship are ultimately dependable.

The interpersonal effects of being so persuaded are far-reaching. Trust in the transcendent enables us to rise above our abandonment/absorption dilemma in relationships and, consequently, our need for defensiveness. "If God is for us, who is against us?" writes Paul (Rom. 8:31), reminding us that our ultimate validation is from God. Peculiar to this trust, however, is its tendency to redirect us to our interpersonal life. Faith in God does not liberate us from people, but reveals our freedom and our formation in our relationships to them, in the joyous discovery of the *we* of *me.*

Questions for Reflection

1. At what times in your adult life have you felt helpless? Did you reach out to someone else for help? Why or why not? Why do we human beings have such difficulty accepting our need for one another's help?

2. Are you able to accept a compliment? When you make a good grade or are rewarded for an accomplishment, do you own it as yours or do you feel undeserving or like an imposter? How can you begin to incorporate the good in life so that you can have confidence in yourself?

3. Some would say that those who cling to a religious faith are really very insecure people who use their religion as a crutch because of their inability to stand alone in this world. Belief in God, they would argue, is a reassuring fantasy based on a glorification of the idea of a protective parent. Would you agree? Why or why not?

6

The Secure Life

What are the characteristics of the secure life? What would the truly secure person be like in his or her behavior and interpersonal style? If not defended, how do these people maintain their equilibrium in their relationships? How do they keep from being overpowered or hurt by other people? If they are not doing unto life what life has done unto them, what supplies their motivation and meaning? Can anyone really live the secure life, or is this just an idealistic dream?

These questions will be addressed below. First, however, let's summarize the steps to achieving security that were set forth in detail in chapters 4 and 5.

The Path to Security

While everyone's journey is unique, the last two chapters presented some fundamental steps on the path to security, which takes us through these internal processes and changes.

1. *Remembering.* We must first engage our memories. It is by remembering that we come to regard our own lives as a story, with certain themes and patterns. This enables us to begin that necessary process of standing outside ourselves so we can realistically examine our lives. Without this step of historical self-examination, we are destined to repeat patterns of interaction blindly and employ our defenses automatically.

2. *Mourning.* Next, we begin the difficult process of mourning. First, we must mourn our actual traumas, those interpersonal wounds inflicted on us when we were young and helpless. Second, we must mourn the loss of what we never actually had to begin with, but which we needed in order to grow our selves;

we must mourn our deprivations. The third and final mourning is the mourning of the loss of our defenses themselves. Mourning involves us in a process of letting go of obsolete defenses, of forgiving the past, and ultimately of renouncing our conviction that life is undependable.

3. *Confessing Our Powerlessness.* We must come to a new acceptance of our powerlessness, our weakness, our helplessness, our neediness. In other words, we must acknowledge that we are insecure and that we are unable to become secure by ourselves.

4. *Accepting Our Dependence.* We must come to accept that we depend on others for the coauthorship of our life. It is a recognition of what the poet John Donne meant when he wrote, "No man is an island." With this acceptance, however, comes the ability to distinguish between *relative* and *absolute* dependencies.

5. *Recovering Our True Self.* We must allow our needs and our talents to surface. This means trusting life again, even though our true self was hurt and forced into hiding. We simply have to give life another chance.

6. *Incorporating the Good.* We need to open ourselves to the good that exists in our story, both in the past and in our present. Opening ourselves to the good in our relative dependencies is helped along by an openness to the absolute goodness of God. We need to receive perfect love. This frees us to recognize and maximize the good in our inevitable connectedness to other people.

7. *Being Persuaded.* This means that we open ourselves to the possibility that in our mundane experience we are also encountering the Holy, and that what we encounter in the Holy is the absolute dependability of God as revealed in God's perfect, fear-bashing love. Being persuaded by the good in our experience and in the shared Christian memory amounts to a new life-governing conviction.

These seven fundamental steps, if undertaken not as a simple formula for defeating insecurity but as the steps in a lifelong journey, lead to a deep sense of security, despite the insecurities of this world. What does life look like for the person who has undertaken these steps?

The Marks of a Secure Person

What does a person begin to look like once he or she embarks on the journey toward security just outlined? Actually, he or she will look quite a lot like before. Basic personality does not change all that drastically. A woman who is an extroverted, outgoing, vivacious person will remain such. A man who is pensive, quiet, and intense prior to becoming a secure person will, in all likelihood, possess these same personality traits once he has begun to deal with his insecurity. Aren't there any recognizable changes? Yes, by all means, but the changes can be subtle, and even when they're dramatic they occur within the particular givens of each personality.

The secure look varies according to the uniqueness of each person. Transformation from insecurity to secure selfhood, although deep and far-reaching in its implications, is not equivalent to a personality transplant. Nevertheless, there is a noticeable difference between a secure, self-assured introvert and a nervous, timid introvert. What happens to our personality once we've begun to relinquish our defenses? It begins to flourish in the soil of a freer give-and-take with our world. When the psychological law of the talon is repealed, sharp edges of personality are contoured and harsh features are softened into an elegance of being. Let's examine several marks of the secure person.

Freedom from Fear

Since fear is the emotional component of insecurity, it stands to reason that the truly secure person will be free from fear. Certain false securities, such as those mentioned in chapter 1, have the effect of trapping and suffocating us. We cling to them, but in reality they possess and control us. A Garfield cartoon captures this fact. Garfield, visiting in a pet shop, opens all the various animals' cages and cries, "Be free! Be free!" None of the pets moves, so Garfield, slamming all the cages shut, cries, "Be secure! Be secure!" Materialism, healthism, addiction, religious absolutism, and the structure of our current life-style can be cages of false security. True security opens the cages and embraces the future.

Freedom to Fail and Freedom to Succeed   The secure person is free to fail without being ashamed and free to succeed without feeling alienated. Some of us simply cannot stand to fail. Secure persons do not regard failure as tantamount to disgrace. They can handle losing the tennis match without total self-recrimina-tion. They don't take the whip to themselves every time they fail to measure up to their own taxing standards of parenthood They do not cease taking risks and accepting new challenges at work simply because they might goof up sometimes.

Having incorporated the "good," criticism does not humiliate the secure person, nor is disappointment ruinous. These men and women can cut themselves some slack during an off day. They have a capacity for self-forgiveness as well as for healthy self-correction. They are capable of disappointing themselves but are not undone in the process. The secure person is free to fail and, in that freedom, to learn from past mistakes and go on with life.

Others of us are even more afraid of success than of failure. This is because with success comes increased self-expectations and, we subconsciously fear, isolation from others. Amanda, you recall, hid her considerable talent under a basket of al-legedly feminine passivity lest she intimidate potential suitors. Relinquishing her self-effacing defense opened whole new vistas of both feminine and professional self-determination. Secure persons, like Amanda, do not have to underestimate capabilities or overestimate achievements. They know their capabilities and accept their limitations. They are not tempted to sabotage them.-selves on the threshold of victory. Because they trust themselves in relationships, feel a deep kinship with their fellow human beings, and sense that their story, even in its successes, is being coauthored by the Author of life, secure persons are free to succeed.

Freedom from the Fear of Abandonment and Absorption
The secure person is nondefensive in interpersonal relationships because he or she is no longer threatened by abandonment and absorption. The defenses peculiar to each become outmoded once a person undergoes the seven-stage process from mourning to persuasion. Such persons become less abandonable because,

while the love of others in their lives is extremely important, they love and validate themselves and know they are affirmed by the love of God. They accept the coauthorship of their lives but retain editorial prerogative and submit to the will and wisdom of the Editor-in-Chief for the final text. They will naturally be concerned when someone important (spouse, best friend, protégé, adolescent daughter) pulls away. They are never so self-contained as to be unaffected by being forgotten, ignored, given the silent treatment, or left behind by someone close. Such dealings, however, do not panic the secure person or cause him or her to coerce another into closeness. Instead, the secure person respects and tries to understand the other's need for distance and searches for ways to keep open the doors of communication.

Likewise, the secure person is "boundaried," not so much by an envelope of skin as by personal integrity, by living within his or her true self. Secure persons know where they stop and the world begins. They respect the boundaries of other people as well. They care about others but do not need to be responsible for or control others' lives. Their caring is noninvasive. They are not so thick-skinned as to be impervious to others' claims, but because of their strong sense of security they are able to differentiate themselves from others. Therefore, they are less likely to become lost or absorbed by another's identity or demands. Old distancing defenses are now obsolete. They accept finitude, being creatures of space and time, because they are confident in their connection to the source of their transcendence. They do not try to stand outside time because they realize that interpersonal relationships shape one's personality and contribute to the liberation and nurturance of one's imprisoned potentials.

The secure person is no longer afraid to commit to another person because others can no longer be overwhelming. Significant others can influence our growth and self-concept even when they hate and misunderstand us, but they are not God. Far from being hell, relationships with others become the crucible for the perpetual self-creation of the secure person, who now realizes that family and friends, and even enemies, play a role on the stage of life in the great theater of redemption, sharing in and contributing to the development of the secure person's character.

Freedom from Fear of the Opposite Sex   Perhaps the most pervasive and influential interpersonal fear is that which men and women feel in relation to each other. We need one another. Men need women. Women need men. We belong to one another. We are the same species, yet sometimes the gender gulf seems an infinite expanse. We are alike, far more alike anatomically and psychologically and spiritually than we are different, yet in moments of frustration during a communication impasse, we'd swear we came from different planets! When we truly connect, our very "otherness" becomes a gracious mystery to enliven and empower us. When we clash in discord and misunderstanding, however, we are capable of horrifying destructiveness.

Secure persons are not afraid of the opposite sex. The secure woman can handle the uncertainties of these times and even welcome the challenge because she is not wedded to stereotyped role definitions of her femininity. The secure man is not so bound by narrow definitions of masculinity that he refuses to experiment with behaviors and responsibilities traditionally assigned to women. Nor does he need to suppress her "masculine" pursuits, those activities once limited by tradition to men only. He does not feel castrated when a woman surpasses him in talent and authority. Likewise, in her security, she does not seek the reversal of the sexual double standard but its abolition. Because she is secure and recognizes that both sexes are struggling through gender ambiguities, she is patient, not militantly eager to pounce on his every residual chauvinism, provided he is, at the same time, striving to embrace equality of the sexes.

Together, the secure man and the secure woman accept and value their differences, forging a common future based on their mutual need and dependence. They do so with a sense of humor and with an ongoing delight in their differences.

The Liberation of Passion   Secure persons are spontaneous and uninhibited in their emotional lives. They know and accept that they are capable of both love and hate and are not surprised to be capable of a wide range of emotions, from rage to pity and from envy to compassion. One of the great disadvantages of the defended life is that our defenses blunt our feelings and, by attempting to suppress fear, tend to anesthetize our emotions. The defensive life puts the big chill on our spontaneity and emotionality. In our efforts to defend against abandonment and absorption, we learn to restrain our emotions, both positive and negative ones. When we harness our anger, we inevitably subdue our warmth. It is not unusual, for example, to encounter a man who reports being mystified by his loss of sexual desire for his mate. Fearing both abandonment and absorption by his partner, he may bury his hurt and anger. Frequently, his impotency is temporary and the result of suppressed anger. Unexpressed anger that feeds an unresolved conflict is a surefire depressant of any sexual relationship!

Anger, appropriately expressed, can actually deepen trust and intimacy and intensify the sexual enjoyment a couple experiences. If my partner expresses her anger openly and in a nonaccusatory fashion, I know she trusts me to hear her and work toward understanding. The free expression of anger, over a spectrum from mild irritation to fury, enhances our marital security because it deepens trust.[1] The effect on marital emotionality is emancipating. If I trust my spouse to handle my anger, just maybe I can trust her with my silliness, my giddiness, my irrepressible joy, or even with my tears of sorrow. The secure marriage, then, is rich and alive with sentiment, not emotionally impoverished or deadened by defense.

The secure person is passionate, and not afraid of emotion. If you are secure in yourself, you can relax in the knowledge that your rage, terror, disgust, guilt, and embarrassment are as human as your humility, sympathy, courageousness, and patience. You are liberated from that dread that is the legacy of the "internalized bad" that inhibits your spontaneity, making you feel uneasy whenever you display emotion.

Incorporating the perfect love which casts out fear "ghostbusts" the bad that has haunted and inhibited you up until now. The secure life is marked not by a dull equanimity but by a passionate, dynamic sense of balance. You are like the high-wire artist. With gyroscopic skill you keep on course, despite eruptions within and pressures from without. The fun of it is that once you trust your balance you can dance or somersault your way across the wire, to the thump of your own heartbeat and the gasping delight of the crowd!

Freedom from Paranoid Interaction with God   Many of us have two theologies, the one we espouse and the one we actually live by. Often, the one we live by is based on a dread fear of God. This is because a confusion of God with the "bad," with someone or some experience from our past, has become our functional theology. It's the one in our guts. "God'll get you for that!" it screams at us from inside.

Why are we paranoid about God? The first reason is that we tend to enlist and use God for our guilt defense against our basic badness. Closely related is our tendency to repeat in our interaction with God the dynamics of a bad relationship or experience from our past. A mother who lost her baby several years ago to Sudden Infant Death Syndrome has felt on guard with God ever since. Cognitively she believes in a loving God who does not punish people by killing their babies. At a deeper level, however, given her own basic sense of unconditional badness (she was abandoned repeatedly by both parents), she wonders when God will strike again. She fears God will take her loved ones if she gets too close to them. She both defends herself against the badness of a world where mothers can lose their infants and "controls" God by never allowing herself to depend too unreservedly on anyone.

Secure persons are not in relationship to a capricious, wild-eyed, punitive deity but have differentiated God, at the gut level, from those who abandon them. Mary achieved this. She had to call off her first scheduled baptism because to be baptized "in the name of the Father" was simply too threatening, given her ambivalent and insecure relationship with her earthly father. When she was finally baptized, it was evidence of her having trusted and distinguished the love of God the Father from that of her dad.

The secure person is free from the unholy fear of God. He or she has but one theology for head and heart, a gut theology grounded in God's grace.

Living in Depth

Closely related to emotional freedom is what I refer to as "tapping your depth." Secure persons are rememberers, interpreters, mourners, clowns. They possess a narrative sense of their lives, an interpretive grasp of continuity with the past. They likewise appreciate the significance of those points of radical discontinuity, those crisis points that seem to be random and chaotic glitches in the story line but come to be understood as milestones, or even as turning points.

Secure persons, furthermore, are not afraid to remember their tragedies. They remember their wounds and mourn the brokenness of life, which wounded them and which causes them also to wound others. They are not afraid to recognize and to confess their sin. They are not afraid because they can mourn. They do not have to "fix it" by being better, stronger, more clever, or saintlier. They are not afraid to feel the tragedy of the gap between what is and what ought to be in this world. Mourning itself, they realize, has an inherent value. Were a woman to do nothing else but cry like a Rachel for all the heartache, injustice, and loss around her she would be performing an invaluable deed. Especially is this so in a society that hates sadness and prefers that we live on the thin veneered surface of meaning, winning friends and influencing people, glad-handing, back-slapping, positive-thinking our way up the ladder of success.

Secure persons are able to be mourners in a "smile and be happy" culture because they know that "Blessed are you that weep now, for you shall laugh" (Luke 6:21b). They derive a quiet contentment from the knowledge that mourning frees them from blindly repeating the past, despite the fact this sets them against a spiritually shallow and numbed society. They know the loneliness and nostalgia that come to those travelers who have left the old universe of childhood forever behind. They rejoice, however, when they realize that the old cycle of family dysfunction, which has passed from generation to generation, has lost its momentum. Instead of being mortified by evidences of the old world—residual chauvinism, depressive tendencies, chronic worrying over little things—they laugh at their idiosyncrasies, at those very qualities which once drove them crazy about their parents and which they now see in themselves. They can laugh because they have also mourned, which itself has opened the way to the future and, thereby, to transformation. Because they mourn and laugh, they have hope for the future. The past has lost its death grip. They can see the new, and they believe in it and nurture it. They know themselves in their spiritual depth, their history and their internal complexity and richness of being.

From Doing to Being

The secure person has undergone a monumental shift in orientation to life, from an emphasis on doing to a groundedness in being. Lacking a secure foundation in being, the insecure person has to be pumped up into being by doing, doing, doing— by achieving, performing, proving, earning the right to be here. Whereas the insecure individual awakens every morning to a compulsive need to hit the ground running in order to get a head start on all those fears, the secure person stretches, yawns, and embraces the new day, grateful to have another opportunity to love and to work.

Our cultural emphasis is on doing rather than being. That is why it is so hard for us to relax, to just sit, contemplate, savor the pleasures, and ponder the meaning of our lives. Our very cultural definitions of the "good life" urge us onward and upward, persuading us that it is by "producing" and making more money that we will find happiness. So busy are we, doing all the things we think we are supposed to be doing, that we don't take time for relationship. We don't have the time! When was the last time you simply enjoyed the quiet company of a friend? When was the last time you spent a day doing nothing in particular?

Our culture's backing of a doing orientation simply reinforces our own psychological defensiveness and our need to master our pain by "doing unto life what life has done unto us." Compulsive doing defends us against our inadequate sense of our being. A secure sense of being is the legacy of a secure infancy and childhood, when our parents wisely responded to our emotional needs and created a foundation of trust in our interpersonal world. As pointed out in chapter 2, however, most of us are not so fortunate as to get this kind of start in life. For most of us, the foundation is cracked by too many experiences of the bad. A fault line runs through it. For the fortunate among us, the basic fault is only a hairline fracture because we had adequate parenting and schooling and peer relating. For others of us, the fault is like the San Andreas, threatening to fragment and splinter us, to separate us from the mainland of our very selves.[2]

Mid-life crisis is for many people the recognition of, and subsequent panic over, the growing crack in the foundation. Even those who by forty have managed to achieve their goals begin to realize they are running out of steam; it is increasingly difficult to find the motivation to forge ahead. We can use the analogy of a building to illumine what is going on with the self in mid-life. It is as if, by forty or so, an individual has built a fine structure, aesthetically pleasing, tall and grand, and architecturally sound, except that there is this fault line in the foundation that weakens the overall structure. The individual has to use more and more psychic energy just to keep the walls of the building up. The wise person knows enough to attend to and repair the foundation before adding on to the building or contemplating, with any enthusiasm, growing and living another three or four decades.

Tom, who wrote "Where Are You, Norman Rockwell?" found himself in this very situation. His self-absorption was the result of his having to be preoccupied with keeping himself going. He did this through a kind of frenetic, compulsive doing. Well rewarded for his conventional accomplishments, Tom sometimes resorted to rather strange methods for proving his mettle. Among them, Tom invented a "beat the clock" game with which he would occupy himself when traveling on business. If his plane was due to leave a given city in an hour, instead of heading to the airport, Tom would tour some museum or other tourist attraction and then, at the last minute, race to the airport. He prided himself on the fact that he had never missed a flight, although on many occasions he was the last person to board the plane just as they were rolling away the boarding ramp. In a technologized, computerized, depersonalizing world, we insecure folk do resort to some rather bizarre methods by which to achieve heroism. Picture poor Tom racing madly through airports like O. J. Simpson as a way of being heroic, proving his manliness, avoiding the emptiness inside. Later in this chapter we will examine how Tom made the shift from a frenetic *doing* to a secure *being,* how he became a true hero, and how you and I can achieve our own heroic stature—a stature that grows out of a secure sense of being rather than frenzied doing.

Mary was also approaching mid-life when she decided to confront the basic fault in the foundation of her being. Her orientation to life was expressed in ascetic religious practices. By subduing her passions and denying her needs, she would, she believed, attain spiritual success and therefore self-worth. Her story illustrates how even religious hyperactive doing can constitute a defense against the downward drag of a faulty sense of being. Mary could never successfully resist the downward pull, and her "works righteousness" actually wore her out. When her personal theology began building on the notion of grace, she began to shift from a doing to being orientation. As she gradually allowed herself to trust in the dependability of God's love, Mary found new energy to handle day-to-day living. Her doing, instead of defending her against basic badness and weakness, grew from a secure sense of being. She discovered the truth in the paradox that by resting in God's love, which repairs the fault in the foundation, we produce more good in life, both in quality and quantity.

Confidence and Creativity

Secure persons, who approach life from a being rather than a doing orientation, are able to assess their true talents accurately. They are confident, not cocky. They know what they can and cannot accomplish. They neither short-change nor overestimate themselves. Their confidence, then, is reality-based—the result of their having remembered their story, mourned their losses, and incorporated the good. They do not need the old defenses that caused them either to hide or to exaggerate their abilities.

Sally, you recall, lacked confidence in her abilities as a mother. Thirteen years of marriage to her former husband, Stan, had been the only period of stability in Sally's life. As a child, she had been moved from pillar to post. She had never been in the same school for more than two years in a row. She had grown up in abject poverty, but now lived in prosperity. Stan had been a very successful businessman, leaving Sally quite secure financially. She was, however, terribly insecure otherwise. She never felt at home in her affluent world. Plagued by gnawing doubts about herself, Sally was convinced that because she had grown up poor there was something she didn't know which other people automatically knew.

Sally was constantly comparing herself negatively to others in her social world, never confident of herself, either as a mother or as a person. Despite extraordinary musical ability, Sally could never sing a solo without first enduring sleeplessness and hours of agonizing performance anxiety.

With Stan's death came a double grief for Sally. She found herself grieving not only the loss of the man she loved but also, in reality, grieving a lifetime of losses and deprivations that had eroded her sense of worth. With the loss of her external source of security, she was challenged to find a basis of security within. This required a season of deep mourning. Next, it involved her in resurrecting her esteem by owning her talent and dispelling the classist notion that her early poverty somehow marked her as forever inferior. She drew courage and comfort from Wayne Oates's autobiography, *The Struggle to Be Free,* identifying with the erosion of self-worth that had been the legacy of his poverty and fatherlessness. She was inspired by his defeat of inferiority and by this reassurance:

> The Word of God, the Logos, the person of Jesus Christ, was my redemption from feelings of inferiority. From then on I felt it a divine imperative never to think of any human being as inferior to me, nor, at the same time, to think of any human being as superior to me. . . . My calling . . . has been gently to take off the cheap price tags people place on themselves and ask their permission to bestow the price tag God our heavenly Parent has placed on us with a love that is more than human love. For this nobody need walk in shame for any reason.[3]

Sally began to grow in confidence as a mother and as a musician. She was freer to perform without the usual self-criticism. She worked to rid herself of that nagging sense of inferiority in social settings and started to blossom like a flower, confident in the soil's richness, in the sunshine and rain life would bring, and in her own power to flourish.

Hope in Weakness

As you have gathered by now, many paradoxes are at work in living the secure life; the whole notion of dropping defenses in the interest of security cuts across the grain of conventional wisdom. Not only is this notion paradoxical, it is radical, which is to say it goes to the roots of human nature and concern. One major expression of the paradox of security is that there is hope in weakness. Paul spoke of this when, explaining that he was finally reconciled to the fact of his "thorn in the flesh," he indicated that God's power is somehow made perfect in our weakness. "When I am weak," said Paul, "then I am strong" (2 Cor. 12:10).

Our macho culture hates wimps. It hates weakness. It clings to the delusion that there exists such a beast as the "self-made person" and insists upon our striving for self-sufficiency. It spreads the lie that self-reliance alone is the yardstick against which we measure our own accomplishment as persons. Basically, our culture does not understand the paradox that there is a hidden power, a strange wisdom, an absurd hope waiting in our weakness. Paul knew it. Having once felt as though he had been "utterly, unbearably crushed" (2 Cor. 1:8) by the vicissitudes of life, he came to be an advocate for the weak. You can almost detect a chuckle in Paul's observation that God, in choosing him, "chose what is weak in the world to shame the strong" (1 Cor. 1:27).

Acknowledging our weakness, our helplessness, our powerlessness is one aspect of the feeling of absolute dependence, which is the same as consciousness of God. Feeling our weakness is what opens us to God and thus to the future. Not strong defendedness but brave weakness is what opens us to the possibility of change. It is the basis of our hope.

Secure persons know they are also weak. They are not ashamed of this fact. They know they are not self-made, but rather that their lives are being coauthored with all their significant others, whose help in life they need. Their consciousness of their weakness opens them not only to help from others but to the source of all hope, to the dependable God who, in the divine "weakness" of the Cross, conquered the world, the dependable God of Love who returns the world to the weak as their safe playground, as their Promised Land.

Security and the Defenseless Life

Can anyone really live a defenseless life? Yes and no. I would not be writing this book if I did not believe that it is possible to cease being governed by an automatic defensiveness in life. On the other hand, I do not want to create unrealistic or unfair expectations. Life is dangerous and difficult. Yielding our defenses is not easy to do. My nose would grow through the binding of this book if I pretended that I have abandoned all my defenses! The struggle for security is a journey of faith, with fits and starts, progress and backsliding.

The Christian faith tells us there was a man once who was defenseless, whose only weapon was his complete trust in God. Jesus' consciousness of his absolute dependence was perfect and unwavering. He was the only one to have actually lived the defenseless life. He is the paradigm of human security. His security, we are told, becomes ours whenever we remember him and incorporate and allow ourselves to be incorporated by him. How does this occur?

Lovers, Heroes, and the Still Small Voice

It is difficult to believe in the God of Christ in these modern times. The drumbeats of secularism, science, and pluralism and the deafening roar of individualism all collaborate to drown out the still small voice of God. It is simply not socially acceptable to dream dreams and see visions, much less to report them and act upon them. I would contend, however, that a person does not have to have seen a vision of Jesus or experienced a miracle to have heard the still small voice of God, even in these deafeningly noisy times. There are those on this religiously flat earth who still seek transcendence. As sociologist Peter Berger, a scientist who eavesdrops on the rumors about God, puts it, "The fundamental religious impulse is not to theorize about transcendence but to worship it."[4]

Some people, particularly those who have begun the journey toward security through remembering and mourning, are actually ambushed by transcendence, even in this modern age. Tom—the author of "Where Are You, Norman Rockwell?"—was driving home from work during one extremely cold, snowy January when he passed several homeless individuals shivering on a street corner. He noticed they had no gloves. "I almost stopped my little MG to give one of them my gloves," said Tom, the self-professed Yuppie, "but then I thought, 'Naw, these are thirty-dollar ski gloves!' " That night, however, Tom tossed and turned and could not sleep. He kept thinking about those people who were out in the cold, with no warm bed to sleep in.

The next morning Tom arranged with a local department store to purchase on time three hundred pairs of gloves, socks, and knit hats. He delivered these items personally to the Salvation Army, the local soup kitchen, and to other helping agencies in his city and took time to get acquainted with some street people. This became an annual project.

During that sleepless night, Tom wrestled with conscience and with Mystery. Later, he found a new way to be a hero in a TV-mesmerized world of diminishing dialogue and of a shrinking stage for dramatic action. Never one to be content as a spectator in life, Tom was overjoyed to discover this new basis for heroism. Moreover, he was ecstatic when he spoke of the exhilarating freedom from his self-absorption brought about by this transformation. Secure in himself, he had been able to make the insecurity of others his personal concern. In the homeless, this nostalgia-ridden man, who knew deep down that you can't go home again, had discovered his connection to a homeless humanity and to a homeless God. "I was shivering and ashamed and abandoned and you cared." Or as the

New Testament records it, "I was naked and you clothed me, . . . as you did it to the least of these my brethren, you did it to me" (Matt. 25:36, 40).

The Theater of Redemption

Like Tom, you and I need to discover ways in which we can be heroic in this high-tech era of mall shopping, mass-produced identities, and shrinking frontiers. Like Tom, we long to stop worrying about ourselves and truly to love others. We want to drop our defenses and throw ourselves into life. You can do this. The secure life is achievable, provided you think of it in terms of a journey, with milestones, victories, and some expected set-backs. You can rest assured that, given future loss and heart-ache, I'll be tempted to eat my words regarding the basic dependability of life in this world. I have been thus tempted in the past and have succumbed to disillusionment and despair. But just as surely as despair comes, there is always this restoration of hope initiated by God. I can't prove to you that divinely initiated love is what it is, but I can describe a way of seeing life and the world and hope to stir in you a kindred imagination.

My favorite theologian is Friedrich Schleiermacher, the nine-teenth-century religious genius whose views concerning the "feeling of absolute dependence" were mentioned in chapter 5. Don't be intimidated by his long German name. Despite his intellectual brilliance, he was a pussycat, a people person from the word go. He realized that life is a coauthorship with God and others. Despite great tragedy in his life, Schleiermacher saw the world as the theater of redemption. It was for him a place where we are all striving toward that greater consciousness of God. It is a secure place, ultimately, because, in Christ, love has won out and will prevail. The God upon whom we depend, he believed, is absolutely dependable. For all its dangers, the world is still a place where a person can experience the love of God. His last act on his deathbed was to serve communion to his friends. He was remembering and mourning and incorporating "the good" to the very end.

Even in his dying Schleiermacher acknowledged his relative

dependence on those around him and theirs on him. His family and friends were, he knew, the *we* of his *me,* coauthors of his story, which was now on its last page. Communion on dying day! That, my friends, is a secure life.

The security of the Christian life is not the rosy-cheeked tranquillity portrayed in a Norman Rockwell painting. The final paradox is that security in Christ actually expands our capacity to live with insecurity in this world. It makes the insecurity of "the least of these" our insecurity. Following Christ will lead us into the cavernous jaws of insecurity over and over again. If you lay down your defenses and follow him you will lose your life. If you keep your defenses, you will die too, albeit possibly with fewer scars. Do you want to die pretty or do you want to have lived?

Think of the world as a great theater. You share the stage with humanity. You and I and all the rest of us are making up the script as we go along, or so it seems. I prompt you. You prompt me. I help you develop your character and you help me develop mine. We do our best to create a sensible, humane plot. We realize, however, that we share the stage at a challenging time in human history, when nothing seems nailed down. The stage floor is shaky and worn, and we trip over one another from our poor choreography. Our voices echo through a hollow theater of endless space. We hear no evidence of an audience, no laughter, no applause. If you're a woman, your role keeps changing. If you're a man you have to adapt to ever-changing cues for your part. No really heroic or distinguishing roles are left. Most parts call for mass-mindedness, greediness, arrogance, and tough-guy hardness. We keep repeating the same tired lines in a meandering plot.

A mushroom cloud has been part of the set since you and I appeared on stage. We were there when the music died. We've witnessed assassinations, atrocities, famine, a televised war, and a zillion commercials. We've been repeatedly betrayed. Worse, we have betrayed others and ourselves. "Out, damned spot!" we cry, but the spot remains.

Although there have been some funny scenes, we realize we are not acting in a comedy. This is a tragedy we're in. We tremble through many scenes, huddled close to our fellow actors, flubbing our lines, having no idea what will come next. Some of us withdraw to some dim corner of the stage, where we can be found crouching, sucking our thumb or crying in our beer, covering our eyes to keep from seeing an unknown future. Most of us are afflicted with stage fright from our first scene to our our final bow. Somebody next to us dies and we all gape and forget our lines. Filled with constant foreboding, we wonder who is responsible for this melodrama. "Author! Author!" we cry, but the playwright never seems to appear. For many of us, this is the theater of the absurd, and we must endure its insanity without losing our own sanity. If we could look back over the entire drama we would see a great crimson river of humanity, ebbing and flowing in great waves across the stage of history. Who are you in all this?

A Christian interpretation is that you are an indispensable member of the cast in the drama of redemption. What appears to be an absurd play is actually God's story and yours, unfolding into grace and hope and love. The playwright is also the lead actor, and the plot has to do with love prevailing. Your role is crucial to the story and to all the other players. In this interpretation lies the basis for your security and mine in this world. It envisions a new script, one filled with meaning and with mercy and justice. It is, after all, not a tragedy but a passion play. The meek, the sorrowful, the powerless are its true stars. In this drama we cast members are gathered together, speaking our different languages and hailing from all nations and from every era, into a great choir. Someone starts to sing and we all join in. What was the wailing of a trembling, insecure humanity becomes song, beginning with "People" and soon, with practice, the "Hallelujah Chorus."

I'll see you at the cast party, if not before!

Questions for Reflection

1. Our culture has generated numerous macho mottoes that reveal a belief in rugged individualism, self-reliance, winning by intimidation, and survival of the fittest, such as Ben Franklin's "God helps those who help themselves" or the more contempo-

rary trio, "When the going gets tough, the tough get going," "Winning isn't everything, it's the only thing," and "Never let them see you sweat!" What are some other mottoes that reflect this spirit?

2. What motto best expresses your deep convictions about life? One of the apostle Paul's mottoes was "When I am weak, then I am strong" (2 Cor. 12:10). How does that sentiment compare with mottoes we hear and ascribe to? What scripture verse best captures your basic conviction about life?

3. Are you operating from a "doing" orientation or a "being" orientation to life?

4. What is your gut theology? Is God's world safe and is God's love dependable? Does your faith perspective increase or decrease your sense of security? How will you alter your personal theology in light of this book's discussion of security?

Notes

Chapter 1: "Where Are You, Norman Rockwell?"

1. Edward Farley, *Ecclesial Man: A Social Phenomenology of Faith and Reality* (Philadelphia: Fortress Press, 1975), pp. 9–13.

2. Psychiatrist Robert Jay Lifton has made a searching assessment of the impact of nuclearism on the loss of a sense of transcendence and the continuity of life in *The Broken Connection: On Death and the Continuity of Life* (New York: Basic Books, 1983).

3. Robert N. Bellah et al., *Habits of the Heart: Individualism and Commitment in American Life* (Berkeley, Calif.: University of California Press, 1985), p. 151.

4. Erik Erikson, *Identity: Youth and Crisis* (New York: W. W. Norton & Co., 1968).

5. Carol Gilligan, *In a Different Voice: Psychological Theory and Women's Development* (Cambridge, Mass.: Harvard University Press, 1982).

Chapter 2: Fear and the Danger of Attachment

1. I have been greatly influenced by the British School of Object Relations, a psychoanalytic school of thought, which posited that the main motivating force in life is toward relationship. We establish a sense of ourselves by and through our relationships. This school held a positive view of dependency and viewed "mature dependence" rather than "autonomy" as the goal for healthy development. Ronald Fairbairn, Harry Guntrip, and Donald W. Winnicott are three of these thinkers whose concepts I draw upon in this and following chapters.

2. The concept of "good enough" parenting comes from Winnicott. Good enough parenting is that which creates an emotionally safe environment, one sensitive to the child's developmental tasks and providing a consistent and, for the child, predictable response to his or her need for touch, space, empathy, boundaries, play, guidance, and attention.

See Donald W. Winnicott, *Collected Papers* (New York: Basic Books, 1958).

3. D. W. Winnicott, *Home Is Where We Start From: Essays in Psychoanalysis* (New York: W. W. Norton & Co., 1986), p. 65.

4. D. W. Winnicott, "Transitional Objects and Transitional Phenomena," *International Journal of Psycho-Analysis* 34:2, 1953.

5. Henry J. S. Guntrip, *Personality Structure and Human Interaction: The Developing Synthesis of Psychodynamic Theory* (New York: International Universities Press, 1961), p. 437.

6. The term "bad" is used by the object-relations theorists in a survival sense, not in its moral connotation. The situation is "bad" for the child emotionally in that basic needs are thwarted, making it difficult for him or her to grow a self. There are two basic kinds of badness. On the one hand, there is the badness of outright rejection of the child's needs by the parent or other caretaker. This may involve rejection of the child as a person, rejection of his or her true self. On the other hand, there is the badness of seduction. This occurs when the parent leads the child to believe a caring response is forthcoming and then withholds love. The child comes to experience such tantalizing seductions as, themselves, painful and untrustworthy.

7. Harry Guntrip, *Schizoid Phenomena, Object Relations, and the Self* (New York: International Universities Press, 1969), pp. 387–388.

8. Ibid., p. 174.

Chapter 3: The High Cost of Defense

1. Harry Stack Sullivan, *The Interpersonal Theory of Psychiatry* (New York: W. W. Norton & Co., 1953), pp. 329–331.

2. William Lynch, *Images of Hope: Imagination as Healer of the Hopeless* (Notre Dame, Ind.: University of Notre Dame Press, 1965), p. 106.

3. Ibid., p. 115.

4. Ernest Becker said that much of our defensive behavior as human beings can be viewed as stemming from the fact that we are creatures who are set apart from the others by virtue of our consciousness of death and our simultaneous need to suppress this consciousness. See *The Denial of Death* (New York: Free Press, 1973).

5. Psychologist Carl Jung referred to our internal bad aspect as the repressed "shadow" that we are capable of denying by projecting it onto someone else.

6. Karen Horney, *Neurosis and Human Growth* (New York: W. W. Norton & Co., 1950), p. 222.

Chapter 4: Opening the Way to Security

1. Sigmund Freud, *Beyond the Pleasure Principle,* trans. James Strachey (New York: Bantam Books, 1959), p. 46.

2. Jane Loevinger, *Ego Development: Conceptions and Theories* (San Francisco: Jossey-Bass, 1976), pp. 341–395.

3. Walter Brueggemann, *The Prophetic Imagination* (Philadelphia: Fortress Press, 1978).

Chapter 5: Trust and the Security of Attachment

1. William Lynch, *Images of Hope* (Notre Dame, Ind.: University of Notre Dame Press, 1965), p. 39.

2. Ibid., p. 41.

3. Wendell Berry, *Home Economics* (San Francisco: North Point Press, 1987), p. 115.

4. Ernest Becker, *The Denial of Death* (New York: Free Press, 1973), pp. 160–170.

5. Friedrich Schleiermacher, *The Christian Faith,* ed. H. R. Mackintosh and J. S. Stewart (Philadelphia: Fortress Press, 1928), p. 16.

Chapter 6: The Secure Life

1. Andrew D. Lester, *Coping with Anger* (Philadelphia: Westminster Press, 1983). Lester offers a cogent Christian reinterpretation of anger from a threat-theory perspective.

2. See Michael Balint, *The Basic Fault: Therapeutic Aspects of Regression* (New York: Bruner/Mazel Publishers, 1968).

3. Wayne E. Oates, *The Struggle to Be Free* (Philadelphia: Westminster Press, 1983), pp. 43–44.

4. Peter Berger, *A Rumor of Angels: Modern Society and the Rediscovery of the Supernatural* (Garden City, N.Y.: Doubleday & Co., Anchor Books, 1969), p. 86.